THE SECRET LIFE OF A SNO

Secret Life Of A Snowbird.com

Lynn,

Greetings from

Arizona.

Len Schritter

2008

The Secret Life of a Snowbird

An Inside Look at Retirement in America's Sunbelt

Hint: It's humorous, poignant and warm!

by
Len Schritter

FIVE STAR PUBLICATIONS, INC.
Chandler, AZ

Copyright 2007, Len Schritter

Linda F. Radke, President
Five Star Publications, Inc.
P.O. Box 6698
Chandler, AZ 85246-6698
Library of Congress Cataloging-in-Publication Data

Schritter, Len, 1950–
  The secret life of a snowbird: an inside look at retirement in America's sunbelt / by Len Schritter. – 1st ed.
    p. cm.

ISBN-13: 978-1-58985-074-3
ISBN-10: 1-58985-074-2

1. Retirement, Places of – Sunbelt States. 2. Retirement – United States – Anecdotes. 3. Retirement – Humor. I. Title.
  HQ1063. 2. U6S394 2007
  306.3'809791 – dc22

                    2007016014

EDITOR: Paul M. Howey
PROJECT MANAGER: Sue DeFabis
COVER DESIGN: Jeff Yesh
TYPESETTING: Jerusalem Typesetting, www.jerusalemtype.com

Acknowledgments

There are so many people I need to thank.

First and foremost to my wife Diana: Without your inspiration and support, I would not even have attempted this endeavor. Thank you so much for everything. You are the love of my life.

To my aunt Carolyn: You were with me from the beginning when this thing was only an idea in my head. Thank you so much for all your encouragement.

To my children, Amie, Josh and Karoline: Whenever I needed a lift during my day, I just thought of you. You are the center of my life.

To my brother Mike: A special thank you for your organization and management skills. You have made Schritter Farms a shining beacon at the end of Desert Road.

To Darryl, Bob, Joe, and Mark: Without your lifetime of loyalty, dedication, and hard work, there would be no Schritter Farms.

To Linda Radke and her talented team of professionals at Five Star Publications: A very special thank you for producing this superbly edited and wonderfully crafted book. Your enthusiasm and hard work has helped to make a dream come true.

And to all those 55 years old and over who still have unfulfilled dreams and aspirations: This book is dedicated to you.

Len Schritter

Table of Contents

These are in fact, true stories. That said, the timeline of events, certain conversations, and some names have been altered to serve the work and protect privacy.

Introduction

RUBBED BY A PIG

"**W**ould you like me to rub you with my pig?"

The female voice jolted me from reading the newspaper sprawled out on the table in front of me. It wasn't so much the voice that startled me, but rather what she said that got my attention. Rub me with a pig? Surely, I must have heard her wrong.

"I beg your pardon?" I asked as I raised my head and looked at the woman sitting across the table from me.

"I said would you like me to rub your dauber with my lucky pig? It might bring you luck tonight."

I found myself staring into the round face of a grey-haired woman who looked to be in her mid-seventies. She wore several beaded necklaces of various colors around her neck and had on a white sweatshirt with the words "Bingo Player" printed in red on the front. An impish little grin complemented the playful twinkle in her eye as she dangled a pink, stuffed toy pig about three inches long next to her right ear.

"Now, Mary, leave that nice young man alone," chided the well-dressed woman with nicely styled red hair sitting next to her. "I'm sure he doesn't want to be bothered with your foolishness."

The expression on the pig lady's face abruptly took on

9

an irritated look as she turned to confront the other woman. "It's not foolishness, Dorothy," she shot back. "Why you know perfectly well that Myrna won a thousand dollars after I rubbed her dauber with my pig."

"Yes, yes, but that was two years ago," Dorothy answered with a smug look on her face. She folded her arms in front of her. "And since then, you have rubbed lots of daubers with your pig and nobody's won a thing."

"Hmphhhh!" Mary grimaced and glared at her friend through narrowed eyes. She looked across the table at me again. "How about it, you feel lucky tonight?" she asked grinning broadly. Once again she dangled her pig in the air.

"Mary!" The other woman scolded.

I decided to jump in before the police had to be called. "Sure, sure, I don't mind one bit," I stammered as I slid the long, ink-filled cylinder used to mark bingo cards over to her.

"Go ahead. Rub my dauber with your pig," I said gesturing with my hand.

Mary squealed with delight as she reached for my dauber and began rubbing her stuffed toy up and down its length, turning it over and over in her hand. With a mischievous smile on her face, she shot a glance at Dorothy which was met with an indignant scowl.

And so began another Wednesday night – bingo night in Snowbird Land.

Chapter 1

WHY WE HEAD SOUTH

The warmth will get you. Yes, it will. It will gently wrap itself around you and soak into your every pore. It will make you feel comfortable, safe, and secure as if you were back in your crib so many years ago clutching your favorite little blanket.

The ocean, too, will get you. Oh, yes it will. The ocean will reach out and grab you by all your senses and pull you into its hypnotic grip. As you look out at the waves rolling in, with the sound of seagulls squawking lazily overhead, and the blue sky spreading out forever from the faraway edge of the sea, time will cease to exist.

It was December and I was in that timeless, magical place so seldom found these days. It's a place where life's complications melt away amid the salty spray against your face and the warmth of the sun on your body. I sat contentedly as wave after wave crashed on the sandy shore in front of me, all my senses soaked in the leisurely peace and serenity of the scene before me.

Just then I caught sight of a lone figure out on the ocean. It was a surfer lying on his board. Intrigued, I sat upright, squinting to get a better look. He lazily paddled at the water as he gazed out at the sea.

As a wave approached, he turned towards the shore

and began paddling furiously. At the exact instant the wave reached him, the surfer stood up and the ocean propelled him forward, his arms held out away from his body for balance.

I was mesmerized by this dance between man and ocean. The giant wave, steel blue against the sparkling sky, rolled forward and acted as the perfect backdrop for the surfer, who slowly rode his board down the cresting breaker, arms outstretched, the sun glistening off his wet skin. In his wake, a ribbon of white water trailed behind him.

He descended down the steep wave while it gradually curled over the top of his head and then hid him from my view. With a predictable suddenness, the wave crested and the surfer and his board disappeared under the white, frothy foam.

I sat forward and waited anxiously. I fully expected to see his head pop up out of the rushing water, or to watch his surfboard suddenly being hurled out ahead of the cascading wave. But I saw nothing.

Then like a jolt, a voice came from out of nowhere, beckoning to me, piercing through the roar of the ocean. At first I did not heed the voice. I tried to ignore it, wanting to keep my focus on the waves in front of me. But it persisted, calling to me, insisting on my attention.

"Hey!"

Startled, I turned around quickly and saw my wife in the kitchen. She was poking her head around the corner and staring at me. Suddenly, the warm sunshine and the sand and the waves all vanished.

"Why aren't you answering me?" she asked, sounding somewhat annoyed. Her short red hair was accentuated by the red pullover blouse she was wearing. She looked at me with her dark brown eyes while she idly dried a glass with a dishtowel, awaiting my response.

"I'm...sorry," I stammered. "What did you say?"

"I was asking if you wanted any more coffee before I threw the rest out. I want to wash the pot."

I glanced down at the end table next to my recliner and saw that I still had half a cup left, my third that morning. "No, I'm fine," I said, looking up and attempting a feeble smile.

She disappeared wordlessly around the corner and back into the kitchen. A bit perturbed by the intrusion, I quickly turned my attention back to the T V. But it was too late. They were already cutting away to a commercial. The female announcer's voice, young and energetic, with tropical music in the background, beseeched me not to change channels.

"Don't go away. The Travel Channel's countdown of the top ten beaches in the United States will continue after this message."

And just like that, the ocean was gone.

A man and a woman appeared on the screen and started extolling the merits of the "amazing adjustable bed," a commercial I had seen a million times. I reached down the side of my recliner and jerked on the wooden handle. The footrest went down with a thud. I stood up and arched my back and stretched my arms. I figured the surfer had to be okay. Otherwise, they would have said something, I said to myself.

I pushed my hands deep in the pockets of my faded jeans and walked over to the large picture window in our living room. I gazed out at the front yard and beyond and sighed. "I mean, they wouldn't show a guy drowning on T V, would they?" I muttered.

It was four days after Christmas. My wife and I had come back to our home in Aberdeen, Idaho from Arizona for the holidays. We'd been busy the last couple of weeks doing the Christmas thing – putting up decorations, Christmas shopping, attending church services and family gatherings, opening presents, and eating way too much.

By the time I finally got the last ornament safely tucked away in its box, I was anxious to see a cactus again. We should have been back in Mesa by now. But here we were stuck.

I looked out the window at the blizzard which was still in full fury. Nearly a third of the picture window was obscured by snow plastered there by the wind. My neighbor's empty potato field across the road from us came into view only sporadically through the gusts of heavy snow blowing past.

I looked at our car and pickup truck parked in the driveway. They looked like two large white blobs. There was a four-foot high drift of snow piled up behind them. Everywhere I looked it was white. I could hear the wind howling from where I stood, my face inches away from the window. There was no sign of life outside. No cars, no trucks, no one out and about. Only the snow blowing hard from right to left past my face.

"And now, back to the Travel Channel's countdown of the top ten beaches in the United States."

I turned around in time to see more sand and surf on the screen. Young people in swimsuits were walking and laughing in the sun while waves crashed on the shore. Oh, how I longed to be there, walking on the beach, feeling the sand between my toes, relishing the warmth of the sun on my face. I turned again and looked dolefully out our front window. The contrast couldn't have been more painful. I felt like I was in prison.

My wife Diana appeared from the kitchen. "I'm going downstairs to check the email now," she said as she walked past. I smiled and nodded as she disappeared around the corner and down the hall that leads to the stairway. At least I was snowed in with Diana, I thought.

As I heard her footsteps clipping down the stairs, I considered how lucky it was for me that we had found each other. The second marriage for both of us, we had our ups and downs as all couples do, but for the most part, we enjoyed a happy marriage. With her fiery red hair and a temper to match, partnered with my easygoing (okay, some might say lazy) manner, living together had on occasion proven to be a challenge.

But now after twelve years of marriage, I felt as if we were finally on a roll. I sensed that our relationship was in full bloom now and we were enjoying each other's company as it was meant to be.

Smiling at the thought, I turned my attention once again to the picture window. As the snowstorm raged on outside, I was reminded of an incident that happened on our trip down to Arizona a few months earlier. A comment I heard back then had stuck in my mind and I'd wrestled with it ever since.

∽

It had been a late Friday afternoon in early November. The mesquite brush and the cacti had been our companions along the side of Highway 93 for the last two hours. The two-lane road – winding itself through the desert and past the tiny towns of Wikieup and Nothing, past the Joshua Tree National Forest, past hillsides covered with the tall saguaro cactus, through downtown Wickenburg and on into the vast city of Phoenix itself – had become the last gasp of a thousand-mile drive. Our two-day trip was almost complete.

I recall that the sun was shining brightly and the sky

was clear. The air conditioner was blowing a gentle, cool breeze over my face and arms. Even though my back ached and my neck was stiff from so many hours on the road, I was relaxed, probably more from anticipation than from anything else.

As we entered the heavy traffic of Phoenix, I glanced down at the radio and pushed the button to turn it on. A traffic report seemed to be in order. There was always one on the radio somewhere down here. The young female voice reported nothing out of the ordinary; a crash on the side of the road here, traffic slowing down there. Our route to Mesa didn't seem to be affected too much, other than the fact that rush hour was fast approaching. I took a deep breath and glanced up into the bright blue sky.

Soon we would be pulling into our winter resort community in east Mesa. Before long, I'd be leaning back on the recliner in the living room with my feet up. No snow. No snow shovels. No icy roads. The closer we got, the prospect of leaving December, January, and February behind us made me feel downright giddy. I imagined how a cold day down here would probably be the equivalent of a cool day in early June for us back home. I relished the thought.

The sun was beginning to set as we entered Mesa. It splashed its dying rays over the wide expanse of the East Valley, casting the surrounding mountains in a brilliant, red haze. We exited the freeway and made our way through the busy streets towards our park.

We were only blocks away when Diana broke the silence. "We should probably stop and get some milk and a few other things before we get there."

"Good idea," I replied, suddenly aware that my stomach was beginning to rumble. "I'll stop at this Safeway up here on the left." I flipped the turn signal down and we pulled into the parking lot.

The Arizona air, still warm from the sun-drenched day, hit us like a hammer as we opened the door and stepped out of the car. Warmth that I hadn't felt for a couple of months enveloped me as we walked through the parking lot towards the store. It was the first time I'd been outside without a jacket or coat for weeks and it was surreal, almost as though we were on another planet.

We entered the store and Diana reached for a cart. I headed for my usual post, a bench over along the wall. There is something about men in a store and a bench. We seemed to be made for each other. As long as there are men who go shopping with their wives, there will always be the need (make that an extreme necessity) for the noble bench.

Shortly after Diana and I got married, I once used the opportunity of grocery shopping to teach my wife about the perils of impulse buying. Bad mistake. Ever since then, the bench has become my trusted friend.

As I strode past the rows of busy checkout stands, I noticed that the bench I was approaching had a lone occupant seated on one end. He was an older gentleman, rather small of stature and dressed very dapper with an attractive cardigan and a golfing cap at a jaunty angle on top of his head.

"May I join you?" I asked.

The man looked up at me with a blank expression on his face and, without saying a word, gestured toward the other end of the bench. I sat down and leaned back, folded my arms, and let out a sigh.

It was the start of the weekend and the store was a whirlwind of activity with long lines at the checkout counters. The little man and I sat there silently for a long time, both of us watching the comings and going of the crowds of people.

Young mothers with small children in tow passed in front of us pushing their heavy-laden carts. Men with dress shirts, their ties loosened in that "end of the day" look, scurried by carrying only one or two items, probably responding to an urgent appeal from home. White-haired senior citizens ambled past with a few meager items scattered on the bottoms of their carts. It was a busy place, and I delighted in watching the diverse cast of characters walk past me.

The elderly gentlemen sitting next to me suddenly began speaking as though he'd just emerged from a trance. This startled me a little bit because he'd not said a word since I sat down. In fact, he'd barely moved. I assumed he was talking to me, but it was hard to tell since he was looking straight ahead and seemed to be talking to some invisible person.

"I just can't believe it," he said, raising his hands in front of him. "I was at a place today that had anything you could ever want to buy – tools, clothes, cleaning supplies, all kinds of stuff, all in these long buildings out in the desert."

I figured he must be talking about the big Swap Meet that was not too far from our house just off the freeway. Diana and I had been there many times on our previous trips to Arizona.

The old man continued, his eyes wide with amazement and gesturing wildly. "Everything you could ever imagine was there, and even some things I didn't know had been invented yet. Me and my daughter walked for hours looking at all the stuff."

For the first time, he acknowledged my presence by turning to me and directing his words to my face. "And you know what?" he asked as he stared into my eyes with a look of complete astonishment on his face. "It all reminded me of the time when I was in Arizona."

Without thinking, I blurted out, "But you are in Arizona."

I immediately kicked myself for saying it. The man's eyes seemed to glaze over and the expression on his face gave way to one of complete confusion.

"I am?" he asked, tilting his head slightly and scratching his head beneath his cap. He turned slowly and began gazing out at the vast expanse of the store in front of him.

For a few awkward seconds, time stood still. With all the hectic activity around us, all the shoppers streaming by our little bench, we became an island unto ourselves in the midst of all the commotion. I sat there feeling very alone with this little man, wishing I'd kept my mouth shut. I forgot that I was in the very center of "retirement universe." People I'd now be rubbing shoulders with on a day-to-day basis would generally be in a different category than the people I saw every day back home in Idaho. I needed to shift into a more sensitive mode, and quickly.

I sat there helpless, watching the old man scratch his head as he tried to make sense of what I had just said. Embarrassed, I couldn't think of anything else to say. Indeed, I dared not say anything more for fear it would only add to his confusion.

Just then, an attractive, middle-aged woman in pink shorts and matching blouse approached us pushing a heavily loaded grocery cart. She stopped at the edge of the bench and looked down at the man, who was still gazing off into space, his face scrunched up in an expression of puzzlement. With a soft smile, she gently placed her hand on his shoulder. That startled him and he jerked his head back as he looked up into her face.

"Come on, Pop," she said. She shot me a quick, analytical glance. "I think I got everything on the list. It's time to go now."

Slowly and with great difficulty, the elderly gentleman, golf cap still askew atop his head, proceeded to pull himself up off the bench. Wordlessly, he shuffled over to the woman's side and put his arm through hers. I watched as she began pushing the cart at a snail's pace, guiding him along towards the exit of the store. They eventually disappeared out the automatic doors and into the parking lot.

This would be the first of many encounters which would serve to remind me of where I was and with whom I would be sharing my space. In my mid-fifties, I was at the early side of that retirement spectrum, just entering into a phase of life that many of these folks were already well into. I was to learn quickly that "people watching" in Arizona was an experience all its own; a sometimes sobering practice that would make me painfully aware of my own mortality.

I was relieved to spot Diana standing in line at a checkout counter a couple of rows over. Thank goodness, I thought, as I got up and walked over to her. The experience with the old man had left me feeling a bit shaken.

"I hope you want pancakes for breakfast," she said as I looked into the cart.

"You know I never turn down pancakes." I visualized sitting at the breakfast table tomorrow and watching the syrup slowly running down the sides of a heaping stack of hotcakes. We started to empty the cart on the belt.

When it came our turn to be checked out, a petite woman in her early twenties with short black hair smiled and greeted us with a warm hello as she began scanning our groceries. She must have seen this picture many times before because, as she slid a carton of orange juice across the scanner, she looked up and asked, "Are you just getting here for the winter?"

"Why, yes we are," I replied. I was startled to think we looked so transparent. "We just pulled into town."

"Where are you from?" she asked over the familiar beeping of the scanner.

"Idaho," I said. "And boy, are we glad we're here. It was really cold when we left yesterday."

Diana nodded in agreement as she waited with her pen poised over the checkbook.

The cashier stopped her work for a moment and the beeping abruptly quit. She glanced quickly from side to side and then leaned over as if she were going to let us in on some great secret. "Well, you know," she said, her eyes narrowing. "It's really starting to get cold here, too. Why, I had to dig a sweater out of the closet this morning before I could come to work." She stood straight up again, continuing with her work and the beeping resumed.

You could almost hear my jaw hit the floor. She was kidding, right? I looked out the window at the far end of the store. Half expecting to see howling winds and blowing snow, I only saw sunshine and people walking through the door in shorts and T-shirts.

What the heck was she talking about? It was obvious this lady was sadly misinformed. I felt sorry for her in a strange way and wanted to set her straight right then and there. Maybe with a PowerPoint presentation, replete with wind chill charts, temperature inversion data, and snow depth analysis, I could show her what cold really was. I didn't get a chance, however, as my wife ushered me out the door.

The short drive from the grocery store to our house should have been a pleasurable one, as the last moments of our long trip were finally here and soon we would be pulling into the driveway. But I was haunted by the cashier's warning which had filled my mind with visions of winters past. As we drove the last few blocks to our park, I found myself muttering under my breath. "It's really starting to get cold outside. Yeah right."

To me, "cold" was standing at the end of our lane every morning with my little brother, waiting to catch the school bus. We would stand there all bundled up like two little penguins, our breath swirling around our heads in the frosty air until mercifully, the bus finally would pull up to us, tires crunching the snow beneath them.

To me, "cold" was driving twenty miles an hour in a long convoy of cars over an isolated, snow-packed and icy stretch of Idaho highway, everyone just inching along, trying to stay on the road. Both of my hands would be on the wheel in a death grip and I would just hope and pray some semi truck wouldn't come barreling up behind me.

And yes, "cold" was standing helplessly at the window of our living room while a raging blizzard kept us trapped inside our own house. We would wonder how long it would be until the fierce winds would die down so that the snowplows could come and start digging us out.

∞

"The Travel Channel's countdown of the top ten beaches in the United States will be right back after this message."

I turned away from the window leaving the snow and wind behind, settling once again into the cushy depth of the recliner. As a large, rotund man on the screen tried to get a young couple to sign a stack of loan papers, my mind wandered.

What does it really feel like to have such blissful ignorance that you actually think anything above freezing should be labeled as cold? I leaned back in my chair and laced my fingers together behind my head. As the man on the screen showed a flash of anguish in his facial expressions because he'd lost another loan to his competitor, a smile crinkled on my face as I began to comprehend a simple and profound truth.

We snowbirds have found in Arizona a heavenly winter's warmth which will never be fully appreciated by those who have no clue…no clue as to what winter can really be like.

Chapter 2

WHAT'S WRONG WITH A LITTLE BURLESQUE?

October was crazy in Idaho with the harvesting of sugar beets and potatoes. This was the month of sixteen-hour days. It was crazy! The roar of diesel engines waking up a red sunrise in the east. All day long, an army of Case 1H tractors would be creeping up and down the fields. Then there were the inevitable breakdowns, worn out bearings, flat tires, along with trucks moving in and out of the fields, bologna sandwiches, satellite radio, dust and dirt, and then sundown. But that did not mean the end of the workday. The nights were filled with bright lights, fueling up, greasing bearings, and then finally heading home for dinner, bed, and then…a red sunrise in the east heralding the dawn of another day like the one just finished.

Hour after hour, day after day, it would go on, seemingly without end. Every day would be the same as the day before. Time would become measured by counting the empty fields that were being left behind. On and on and on it would go. And all the while, in the back of my mind, there would be the promise of November. There would be Arizona.

Eventually, we would get done. The last potato would drop onto the pile in the storage building, the last sugar beet would be pulled out of the ground, and it would be over. The long year of planting, cultivating, watering, and harvesting would come to an end.

I was sitting on the edge of our bed, packing for our trip down south. It was early November. Harvest was now blessedly over. But now, I couldn't find my shorts. I had looked everywhere – dresser drawers, closet shelves, and storage boxes. They were nowhere to be found. I was on the verge of panic. Just like American Express, I could not leave home without them.

Shorts defined me in Arizona. I rarely wore them at home in Idaho. Ah, but down there, that was a whole different ballgame. It never took very long for my dazzling white legs to be transformed into a nice golden brown. It was cool to have bare legs in Arizona. In fact, it was almost required.

I could have made all this much easier, I suppose, if I'd just left them down there all year long. After all, Arizona was practically the only place I ever wore them.

But each year would be the same. I would vow that this would be the year that I would come out of my shell and muster up enough courage to wear them around my hometown. Maybe even wear them into the town's only coffee shop. Now that would turn some farmers' heads.

It never turned out that way. Oh, I would gather all my shorts up and bring them with me all right. Once back home, however, I would quickly slip back into farmer mode. Which meant a "farmer's tan" wouldn't be far behind.

Where did I put them after we got back last spring? I had no idea.

I sat on the edge of my bed and looked out the window. It was a cool, crisp late afternoon. Most of the front yard was covered with amber leaves that had fallen from a row of Russian elms that lined the east side of our house. Two crows were picking at something on the bare ground on the edge of my neighbor's field. And in the distance, I could see a John Deere tractor slowly making its way across that same field, pulling a six-bottom plow. The landscape was in fall's inescapable grip.

I looked around the room. I didn't really know where to look next. It seemed I'd exhausted all possibilities. I sighed deeply and bowed my head in defeat. It always seemed to happen this way. There was only one option. The final option. As much as I hated to do it, I'd have to ask Diana.

I heard her footsteps coming down the hall. This would be my chance. Trying to sound as nonchalant as I could, I said in a loud voice, "Honey, have you seen my shorts? I can't find them anywhere."

Diana appeared in the doorway, her tan face framed by her tousled, red hair. She was holding a box full of stuff with both arms and was looking at me as if I had just asked if the earth was round. "Why yes. I've already packed them. They're in the big suitcase." She disappeared quickly, hurrying down the hall.

I remained seated for a moment, staring openmouthed at the now empty doorway. Had I just dreamed that? She said she'd already packed them?

A small chuckle rumbled up from my chest. Well, well, the mystery was solved, all this searching and worrying for nothing. I shook my head. The next thought that crossed my mind was; where had they been? But I wasn't about to chase down the hall after Diana and ask her. That would only exacerbate the situation and make me look even dumber than I already felt. Nope, better off to let sleeping dogs lie. Move on to something else.

I got up off the bed and looked around. Now, where were my sneakers?

The next morning dawned with a crisp bite in the air.

My breath swirled around my head and I could feel the cold chill penetrating my clothes and burying itself deep into my bones. My teeth chattered as the glacial air flooded into my lungs with every breath. I began the long process of loading up the car. I carried boxes. I carried suitcases. I carried bags and bundles. Slowly, inexorably, the trunk and back seat became crammed full with all our stuff. Finally, the last item was shoved into the only remaining space available, and we were off.

Whenever I drive long distances, I am focused like a hawk, my eyes staring straight ahead and my hands taking up the two and ten o'clock positions on the steering wheel. In the driver's seat, conversation becomes a chore for me, interrupting my concentration and throwing me off my center of attention. Unfortunately, this makes me a terrible traveling partner on a road trip.

Diana, realizing this early on in our marriage, adjusted very nicely to this rather boring aspect of our relationship. She wisely uses her time in the passenger's seat of our car to expand her knowledge by delving into the printed word. Books and magazines are her constant companion on our trips in the car.

The first few miles were ridden in silence, as was the custom. I drove while Diana took her position in the passenger's seat with her book in her hands. Empty potato fields and newly tilled farm land glided past our window as we headed south. The few trees that stood alongside the highway were quickly losing their golden leaves.

About ten minutes into the trip, the checklist began.

"Did we remember to turn off all the lights?" I asked.

She looked up from her book. "I think so. I remember checking most of them before we left."

"Okay. Good." I turned my attention back to the road.

A short time later, the doubts came crashing through again.

"How about the thermostat? Did you remember to turn down the thermostat?" Diana asked. She had a worried look on her face.

"Yes, it was one of the last things I did before we left."

She smiled and returned to reading her book.

A long silence ensued. The fall countryside drifted past in a picturesque display of colors and shades. I was just beginning to relax, thinking that all our doubts had been resolved, when Diana suddenly closed her book in her lap. "The coffee pot. Did we remember to turn off the coffee pot?"

I gripped the steering wheel more tightly. "I don't know. Didn't you turn it off?"

"I don't remember," she said, slowly shaking her head. A confused look crossed her face. "Maybe we should go back."

"I'm not going back," I muttered. I had visions of us returning to our house two or three more times during the day and ending up sleeping there for the night. "Don't you think we got the kind of coffee pot that turns itself off?"

"I don't know," she replied softly, staring out the front windshield. Her eyes remained full of worry. "Maybe we should go back."

"Look, I'm sure it's going to be all right. One of us always remembers to turn off the coffee pot. Let's just forget it and try to enjoy our trip."

Diana looked at me for a few seconds and then shrugged her shoulders. The worried look on her face slowly receded as she opened up her book again.

Another long stretch of silence followed while the peaceful landscape sailed by effortlessly. The sky was a deep autumn blue, and a few clouds billowed in the east, hanging lazily over the tranquil scene. It was the kind of day that should have brought peace and contentment into my soul. It was a beautiful, sunny day. We were going to Arizona. All should have been right with the world. But as I now drove down the highway, all I could see were smoke and flames and fire trucks, firemen in their heavy coats and firemen hats scrambling around our yard with hoses and a huge stream of water pouring onto our house as it goes up in flames.

I blinked my eyes and shook my head, trying to make the mental picture go away, but it would not. I glanced down at my cell phone, making sure it was turned on and charged up when the fire department would call to tell us that our house had just burned to the ground.

I looked over at Diana. She was now asleep, her head resting on the window, her book about to fall from her fingertips onto the floor. She was a picture of pure contentment. I looked out on the highway as it stretched before me, but all I could see were flames.

Our car continued over Interstate 15, over Malad Pass, across the Utah line, and past the tall, magnificent Wasatch Mountains that dominate the eastern skyline of northern Utah. It wasn't until we were sitting at a table and looking at menus in a Cracker Barrel more than two hundred miles from home that I felt we were safe. I began to relax and put behind me the vision of fire trucks and smoke. Surely, we would have been notified by now if our house had been reduced to ashes.

Cracker Barrel was like a magnet to our car. Even though Diana had a hard time reading something on our TV screen from her recliner, she could point out a Cracker Barrel billboard from her passenger seat a mile away like a champion hunting dog setting a point on a distant pheasant.

Once the quarry had been spotted, I would dutifully pull off the interstate at the appropriate exit and the adventure would begin.

The crowd in the restaurant was sparse, too late for breakfast and a little too early for lunch. We sat at our wooden table with the old style high-backed chairs as we looked over the menus. We hadn't eaten yet that day and this would be our breakfast.

My eyes skimmed down the list of entrées: Old Timer's Breakfast, Grandpa's Country Fried Breakfast, and Momma's Pancake Breakfast. So named, I suppose, to evoke feelings of nostalgia and longings for a simpler time. It made me feel as if I had just come in from plowing the back forty with my mule, ready to wolf down a quick plate of grits before heading back out to the field.

Our waiter, a nicely groomed young man with a nametag that said "Bob" fastened to his brown Cracker Barrel shirt, appeared at our table. "Have you folks decided yet?" he asked as he smiled down on us benevolently.

Diana reveled at these opportunities. For her, ordering from a menu was not just a simple matter of deciding what she wanted to eat. It had evolved into an intense interrogation of the restaurant staff.

"How thick is your thick sliced bacon?" she asked as she scrunched her face up into an expression of indecision and pried her eyes from the menu to look up at the waiter.

The young man looked stunned. He stammered to find words to describe the thickness of bacon. "Uh…I would say…" He held up his hand with his thumb and forefinger spread ever so slightly apart. "About like this."

"Hmmm." Diana winced as she looked back to the menu. "And how about your eggs, how fresh are your farm fresh eggs?" She lowered the menu and looked back up at the waiter.

The young man seemed to be caught off guard by the intense grilling. Searching for words to describe the freshness of eggs he replied. "Well…uh…as fresh as we can get them." He was no longer smiling. He had a deadpan expression on his face as he stood there with pen poised over his pad, waiting to write down something, anything.

"Hmmm." Diana scrunched up her face again. "Let me see." She continued to scan the menu as she softly bit her lower lip in concentration. "Oh, I'll just have the fruit plate," she said as she closed the menu and handed it to the waiter.

"Very good," he said, breathing a sigh of relief and furiously writing on his pad. "And you, sir?"

"I'll have Uncle Hershel's Favorite, over easy with ham," I said resolutely and without hesitation.

"Very good. That will be right out." His smile returned as he gathered up the menus and left.

I sat back in my wooden chair and looked around the room. As my eyes wandered from the butter churns, flour sacks, and old elixir bottles that were stuck to the walls, one question kept creeping into my mind. Who the heck was Uncle Hershel?

Cracker Barrel's ambiance gave you the impression that there was this old rickety farmhouse out back where a withered old man (no doubt Uncle Hershel) was running around like crazy, slopping hogs, and gathering eggs just to supply this place with all of its raw products. But every time I had ever left one of these restaurants and happened to drive around back, all I'd ever seen was a Holiday Inn and a couple of cooks leaning against a dumpster having a smoke.

After finishing our meal, we headed back through the gift shop to the cashier. This was where the most challenging part of the "Cracker Barrel" adventure takes place. I wish I had been the intern at corporate headquarters who had come up with the idea of putting a gift shop between the dining area and the parking lot. Whoever it was probably has the keys to the executive washroom right now.

Coaxing a woman through that gift shop and out into the car without her buying something is humanly impossible. Diana and I have lots of plunder to prove it, too. Our house has closets full of dancing Santas, singing snowmen, and cuddly bears. I finally resigned myself to that inevitable purchase and after paying the bill I now take my place with the other husbands and wait out front in the rocking chair lineup.

We made it to Las Vegas that night, checking into our hotel room and settling in for a mini-two-day vacation before we would continue on our way to Arizona.

The next morning, after Diana and I had stuffed ourselves at the breakfast buffet, we both took off on our own for a little while. I wandered through the maze of slot machines in the casino and Diana headed for the gift shop.

I soon laid claim to a slot machine on the end of a row and sat down to try my luck. Two machines over to my right sat an old, thin lady with a flowery dress. She sat mesmerized in front of her slot machine, while a cigarette poked out of her lips dangling a long, tottering stem of ash.

Eventually, the dizzying sight of cherries, diamonds, and watermelons spinning round and round endlessly in a successful effort to suck money out of my wallet became too much to take. Thirty minutes and two twenty dollar bills later, I'd had enough and took off on a stroll through the forest of slot machines to find Diana.

I meandered through the casino passing row upon row of these aptly named one-armed bandits. It was midmorning and the place was nearly empty. Only a handful of gamblers were scattered here and there, sitting in front of the slots. As I walked on the soft carpeting, I would occasionally hear the ringing of a nearby machine and the clanging of coins falling, announcing the good fortune of some lucky winner.

Then something caught my eye. Off to my right I saw a flash of color and turned to see what it was. I was met by a large poster. A pair of sexy legs towered above me. I stopped, mouth agape. The caption on the poster read:

CELEBRATING BEAUTIFUL WOMEN
AND THE ART OF THE NUDE

I had quite by accident stumbled upon the entrance to the casino's burlesque show. Now that was something I didn't see everyday out on the farm.

I was curious but cautious as I approached the box office. I looked around to see if anyone was watching. A professional looking, well-dressed young man was sitting at the counter reading a book. I wondered if his mother knew what he did for a living.

He looked up and smiled as I approached the window. "Can I help you?"

"Uh…yeah, I was interested in your show." I squirmed. I fidgeted. The palms of my hands were sweaty. "Is it…uh? Do they…uh?" I didn't know what to say exactly and I tried not to look directly into the man's eyes.

"It's a very well done nightly show imported from Paris," the man interrupted, sensing my discomfort. "It's done in the finest Parisian tradition of burlesque." He said this as calmly as if he were a bank teller helping me make a withdrawal.

"I see." I stood there looking at him dumb-faced. An awkward silence ensued.

"I'm sure you'll enjoy it," he said smiling. "Oh, and you get two cocktails with the show."

I found it odd that he would add this at the end of his pitch, as if I needed an added incentive to see beautiful, naked women. "Okay," I said slowly, looking at the man now. "But is it…? Do they…?" I stammered trying to find the right words. "Could I take my wife?"

The man's face lit up in a look of recognition. "Oh yes, yes. Don't worry about that, sir. This isn't your run of the mill raunchy strip club show. Oh, no no no. This is high class stuff, precision dance numbers, beautiful music, high tech lighting. Lots of couples will be in attendance. Can I put you down for two?"

I stared into the man's eyes through the box office window. His smile seemed to be plastered on his face. My mind began racing a mile a minute. I felt a disembodied hand reach for my wallet in my back pocket and a voice from another world spoke as I felt my lips move. "Uh, sure, why not? I'll take two tickets." Nervously, I handed him a credit card.

My heart pounded in my chest like a sledgehammer hitting an anvil as I raced through the casino towards the gift shop. What had I done? How was I ever going to explain this to Diana? I began rehearsing my sales pitch in my mind as slot machines blurred past me. Guess what, honey? We're going to a high class Vegas show. Beautiful women dance around under special lights to exotic music. You'll love it! Oh, one more thing. They won't have any clothes on.

I caught a glimpse of Diana just as she was coming out of the gift shop. She didn't see me at first and when I got up to her I tried to sound as cheerful as possible. "Don't make any plans tonight." I beamed the biggest smile that my face could produce. "We're going to a show."

"What kind of show?" Diana looked at me suspiciously.

"Oh, nothing special really, it's just a dance show."

I could tell by her expression that she was beginning to smell something fishy. "What *kind* of a dance show?"

"Well, you know, some women dance around on a stage."

"You don't mean one of those burlesque shows, do you?"

"Well," I stammered, "I guess that's what they're called."

Her face contorted into one of horror. "I'm not going to one of those. I'd be the only woman there!"

"Oh, it's not like that at all," I tried to reassure her. "The man at the ticket window said that it's a classy show that lots of couples go to."

"I can't believe you did that without asking me first," she shot back. "Whatever made you think I would go to something like that?"

I could see it slipping away. I had to think fast. "They'll give us two drinks," I said, in a feeble attempt to up the ante.

"I'll need more than two drinks if I'm going to something like that."

Aha, a crack in the door, I thought. I could see myself pouring alcohol down her throat all afternoon if that's what it was going to take. I proceeded to give the door a big kick.

"Hey, this is Vegas," I reasoned. "Don't you think we deserve to live it up a little?"

I could see a slight smile flicker across her face. It was like a sliver of sunshine poking through the clouds. "All right," she said. "But I really wished you had asked me first."

"Oh, I promise, next time I will." I nodded my head apologetically. Outwardly, I remained calm. Inwardly, however, I was pumping my fist in the air in victory. I couldn't believe what had just happened. I had just convinced my wife to sit at a table next to me as we watched a bunch of beautiful naked women dance around in front of us. How did I ever pull this one off? Suddenly the potato fields seemed very far away.

That evening, the showroom was filled with couples of all ages, there to broaden their horizons just as we were. I hate to admit it, but the show itself was rather dull. Oh, there were lots of beautiful women dancing with impressive precision and an eye-popping display of colorful lights blinking here and there all over the stage. The sound system and the music was first rate with plenty of disco-type songs that emitted a great deal of energy. And, of course, there were a lot of boobs. More boobs than you could shake a stick at, in fact. After a while, they just seemed to be incidental and the dancing was what you noticed the most. Honest!

Diana seemed to be enjoying herself though and, as we were leaving, I asked her what she thought of it.

"Well," she said. "Considering that this is Las Vegas, the show wasn't all that bad."

I felt relieved. After all, this was all my doing and I didn't want her to be upset.

But then she added with a twinge of sarcasm. "But I wouldn't take my mother to see it."

Chaper 3

OUR WINTER COMMUNITY

The man seemed oddly out of place. I noticed it right away while I sat there sipping my coffee. Unlike the previous speakers who'd come before him, the short man in the blue windbreaker had a stern look on his face as he stepped forward and grabbed the microphone.

He wore a pair of glasses and had a close–cut gray beard. A deep red complexion added to his already unsympathetic facial expression. And there was something else about him, too. He had a military bearing about himself. Obviously a strict disciplinarian, this man was not up there to mess around. This was not going to be the usual jovial announcement inviting us to join in on the fun. Oh no. This guy had a chip on his shoulder and he meant business.

It was Thursday morning coffee hour, a weekly fixture at the winter resort community in which Diana and I lived. The big ballroom was filled with several hundred "be-backs" – people like us who'd said last spring that they would be back and here we all were. Everyone had been busy getting reacquainted after the long summer's absence. The mood had been light and the atmosphere cheerful. All who were there had been enjoying donuts and coffee and listening to weekly announcements from anyone who wanted to make one.

"Don't miss the computer club meeting every Thursday."

"Painters, the weekly art class will be held in the crafts room the same time as last year. Don't miss it."

"Needlepointers, don't forget to meet every Wednesday afternoon in the card room." And so it went.

It had been almost seven months since I had last attended one of these meetings and it was as though I'd never left. I was looking at a lot of the same faces, listening to the same announcements about the same activities by the same people. It was Groundhog Day redux, Arizona style.

Just when my "sameness quotient" for the morning seemed to be on the verge of going through the roof, the man in the blue windbreaker took the floor.

He looked out at the audience for a few seconds and then lifted the microphone up to his lips. "Does anyone know what this is?" he barked, holding up what looked like a small green baggie. He dangled it in the air for all to see while he stared out at us with an unmistakable look of frustration on his face.

Everyone in the audience looked at the green baggie. Then we looked at one another. Was this a test? A riddle? A joke perhaps? I grabbed for my coffee mug and took a sip of the hot liquid. I was perplexed. I didn't know what he was holding. Nor did I know why he was looking at us that way. What was he up to? I shrugged my shoulders and set my coffee cup back down on the table and wondered what would happen next.

"I see there are no hands in the air," the man continued, still holding the green baggie above his head. "No one seems to know what this is. That disappoints me greatly." And with that, he slowly lowered his arm and tossed the green baggie onto the table beside him.

It became eerily silent in the ballroom. I sat forward in my chair. Out of the corner of my eye, I could see the steam swirling up from my coffee mug. I stared at the man up front as a restless feeling started to permeate the crowd.

He took off his glasses and rubbed his eyes for a few seconds as if he were biding his time, carefully calculating what he was going to say next.

"Let me ask you this question," he said finally, putting his glasses back on. "How many here are dog owners?"

A great many in the audience held their hands up; some of them, I thought, a little too enthusiastically for their own good.

"Well, I see that a lot of you are. Okay, you can put your hands down now."

Like a precision drill team, dozens of hands went down immediately.

The man took a deep breath. I could tell that he was having a hard time deciding how to proceed. "Ladies and gentlemen, I don't like to be hard ass. But I have a complaint."

He stared at the floor and began to pace slowly back and forth as he spoke, the microphone held close to his mouth. "I like living here. I really do," he continued. "I pay my rent, attend the homeowners meetings, and participate in most of the functions here at the clubhouse."

"I try and do my part to keep this park a nice place to live, for everyone." He lifted his head and looked out at the audience. For the first time since he had taken the floor, a crooked smile creased his lips.

"But when I go outside every morning and see that someone's dog has left a nice gift in front of my house? That is where I have to draw the line."

You could have heard a pin drop. People began looking at one another, analyzing their neighbor, perhaps wondering if they were seated next to the perpetrator. Muffled coughs could be heard as a thick uneasiness spread throughout the crowd.

Once again, the man picked up the green baggie from the table and held it high in the air.

"This, ladies and gentlemen, is a pooper bag. You can buy them at your local pet supply store. There are several such stores at various locations within a short ten-minute drive from here."

This must be something new, I thought. I had never heard of a pooper bag before. We were really learning something this morning, whether we had a dog or not.

"These bags are specifically made to pick up after your dog," he continued, dangling the green plastic baggie in the air. "They are scented for your comfort. They even come in several different colors. And they are designed so that your hand never comes into contact with the...uh, offending dog waste."

I grimaced and pushed my donut to the side. What he was describing did not impart a pleasant mental picture for so early in the morning.

"All you have to do is put your hand into the bag, pick up the...uh, offending dog waste, and then turn the bag inside out and tie it shut, and deposit it in the nearest trash receptacle."

I could swear my olfactory nerves were kicking into gear as I visualized the sequence described. I covered my nose, and my eyes started to water.

But some in the audience were really into it. Dog lovers, I presumed. They were leaning forward, their eyes wide in amazement. Some scattered oohs and ahhs could be heard throughout the room as the man pulled on the handles of the bag and it tied neatly shut. I felt as if I were watching an infomercial.

"You see, there is nothing to it." And with a flourish, the man tossed the green baggie back onto the table.

"So in conclusion," he continued, squaring his body to the audience, "to the person or persons who continue to see fit to leave a nice little gift in front of my house every morning…"

People glanced nervously around the room, half expecting the guilty party to stand up and beg for forgiveness, unburdening his or her soul with a contrite heart and a tearful admission of guilt. But no one moved. No one said a word.

"As I have demonstrated, there simply is no excuse." The man in the blue windbreaker was on a roll now. Like a preacher admonishing his flock, he held out his hand and concluded his summation with dramatic clarity. "I implore you, whoever you are – and you know who you are…"

People were squirming in their seats now.

"…do the right thing. Buy a box of pooper bags. Take pride in your park. I thank you."

He lowered the microphone, put his feet together, and bowed to the audience ever so slightly at the waist.

For several long seconds, no one knew how, or whether, to respond. People had blank looks on their faces. Then, as if on cue, they erupted in a thunderous ovation as the man, with a dignified air about him, strode back to his seat and sat down. The enthusiastic applause went on for some time. I half-expected a bouquet of flowers to be tossed in the man's direction any second. Just when I thought he might stand up and take another bow, the applause died down, and the program continued on.

But there was no topping that performance. That would be the announcement of the day. Spellbound by it all, I felt as if I had just watched Gregory Peck deliver his closing argument to the jury in *To Kill a Mockingbird*. I had to fight the overwhelming urge to run right out to the pet store and buy me a box of those pooper bags right after the coffee hour was over, despite the fact I'd not owned a dog in twenty years.

The rest of the meeting was uneventful. Even afterwards, I couldn't stop thinking about the man and his pooper bags. He had been very clever in his approach to the problem, using the culture of a close-knit community to his advantage. Where else could you potentially face an unknown antagonist by addressing a captive audience?

In a strange way, the man with the complaint seemed to bring to light both ends of the spectrum of what living in a resort community is like. On the one hand, you had the close-quarters aspect to it, which brings to bear problems such as the man described. But on the other hand, the proximity of all the residents and the built-in opportunity to tackle serious problems over a cup of coffee gives everybody a chance to resolve their disputes in a spirit of camaraderie. I was beginning to see all the possibilities. Coming to Arizona was like turning off a switch.

Why, it hadn't been more than a couple of weeks earlier that worrying about dog poop would have seemed, I don't know, silly?

I was in another world back then. A thousand acres of potatoes were in the ground and freezing weather was just around the corner. There was a bottom line at stake. Everything we'd worked so hard for all summer long was wrapped up in a short window of opportunity. The success of the coming harvest depended upon many factors that were out of our control – weather, mechanical problems, etc. The stress level on a daily basis was on high alert. Needless to say, back then, dog poop was not on my radar.

After the meeting, I went home, laced my fingers behind my head, and leaned back in the cushion of the patio chair. Harvest was behind me now, and I was at peace. Yes, if a little pile of dog poop was the biggest problem I had to worry about down here, then life would be very good indeed.

As long as there is sunshine and retirees, there will be retirement resort communities like the one we live in. They provide security and privacy, while at the same time offering a variety of activities. If you are bored to death in one of these places, it's your own fault. It's like going to summer camp, except backwards. You go in the winter. And the counselors are the kids and the campers are the old people.

The entire experience begins with the reception at the front gate. Our park must have spent a fortune on sending their guards off to smiling school. Apparently, smiling was their biggest assignment. They smile at you when you drive your car up to their little guardhouse. They come out of the door and they smile. They see your little sticker on the windshield and they smile. They push a button, the gate opens, and they wave you through with the biggest smile you have ever seen. Just what is going on in that guard house? Maybe I should be a guard.

Once you have made it through the smile fest at the gate, your senses are treated to the lush surroundings that most of these places strive to maintain. Palm trees, exotic shrubs, flowers, an array of tall saguaro cacti, and well-trimmed bushes all contribute to the eye-popping sight that greet the winter visitor. A few minutes driving around these parks and you soon forget about the blizzard back home.

There are rules, of course. There are always rules. To keep these winter resort communities looking nice and attractive, one of the biggest rules management puts into place concerns weeds. Weeds are bad. Weeds are not our friends. Weeds are to be controlled, or preferably eliminated, in an expeditious and prompt manner by said property owner. I call it the weed rule. It's become the bane of my snowbird existence.

There was one thing that I quickly learned when I started living down here. The weed rule and procrastination did not mix. They were a lethal combination.

Later that day, long after the coffee hour had concluded, I headed out the front door again to go back up to the club-house. As I opened the door, an unwelcome visitor greeted me by falling down at my feet. A white envelope landed there on the cement walk. Yes, it was the dreaded weed letter.

"This is to inform you that upon inspection of your prop-erty, it was determined that you have not been judiciously complying with the ordinance of the park concerning the control and management of weeds. Please see to it that this matter is taken care of promptly and in a responsible man-ner. Thank you."

Blood drained from my face. I felt as though I'd been sent to the principal's office. Not again! I took a deep breath and glanced quickly at the ground near me. It had been a while since I'd last looked around our place for any weeds. But on this quick inspection from the landing on the front door, I couldn't see a weed in sight.

I looked down at the letter again. Apparently, someone had seen something. I went back inside, taking the letter with me.

Diana was sitting on the couch reading. "I thought you were going up to the clubhouse," she said, looking up from the newspaper.

"I was, but I forgot to do something."

"What's in your hand?"

"Oh, nothing, just some ad."

"What kind of an ad?"

"I don't know. I think it's for weed killer."

I rushed past her and headed for the garage, crumpling up the envelope and the letter. Once there, I tossed the paper into the wastebasket and started opening up drawers and cupboard doors in a frantic search for the plastic bottle of weed spray. I began rummaging through everything I could find. Christmas lights, old golf clubs, and stadium seat cushions all fell at my feet. I know it's in here somewhere, I told myself. Where is it?

I looked from cupboard to cupboard and drawer to drawer. I moved, I scooted, I slid all manner of stuff this way and that, but still nothing. I was coming up empty.

Just when I thought I would have to jump in the car and go buy some, I saw it. Tucked away behind a large coil of orange extension cord, was the small, white and green bottle. "Aha." I snatched it up as if it were a fumbled football and headed out the garage door.

Because of the desert environment in Arizona, the grounds surrounding people's homes often have decorative rock instead of grass. Our house had crushed white rock, each piece no bigger than a couple of inches long, covering the front yard. It was attractive. I had always liked it. And the white rock was an easy contrast against emerging green weeds, making them easier to spot. But in this instance, the weeds were nowhere to be seen.

I stood in front of our house with the bottle of weed spray in my hand, scanning the white rock again and again. Nothing. I worked from right to left, my gaze slowly moving over the white stone, square inch by square inch, looking for any hint of a different color, a contrasting shade, a green weed. Again, nothing. What in the world? Where are the weeds they were throwing such a fit about?

Then, out of the corner of my eye, I caught a glimpse of something. I got down on my knees and bent over a small green plant that was beginning to push its way out from under the rock. It was a little, leafy stem less than two inches tall and barely visible through the thick cover of white rock.

This is it? This is what they're complaining about? I pointed the bottle in the direction of the weed. *Pshhhh.* It never had a chance. I relentlessly squirted, over and over again. The white foamy liquid covered the weed, smothering the defenseless little plant in a continuous gush. I was drunk with power. I felt like emptying the entire contents of the bottle onto the offending weed, but eventually I came to my senses.

Standing up, I surveyed my work. A small foam mountain stood above the white rock. There was no sign of a weed anywhere. It was a job well done.

A few minutes later, my day had resumed and I was on my way again, walking along the familiar street of our park. It was a very warm day and I could feel the heat of the sun on my shoulders.

I loved walking in our park. It was somewhat of a relief from the country living back home where running an errand involved a thirty-mile drive. In our community, you walked. Bingo, exercise room, special events, dinners, lounging at the pool, getting the mail; I wore a path going back and forth all the time.

Just as I rounded the corner and headed east toward the clubhouse, I saw a familiar sight. Virgil was standing in his yard. An old retired farmer from Minnesota, Virgil had to be well into his eighties and was a common sight on this street. He was always outside in front of his house doing something. There was still too much of a farmer inside of him to sit around in his house and do nothing. Each time I would walk past, I could always count on a cheerful greeting and a short visit.

As I approached, he ambled over to the side of the street in his slightly bent-over way. A pair of faded bib overalls hung loosely over his tall, thin frame and a few tufts of gray hair poked out from underneath a well-worn cap.

"Well, how's the potato man?" he asked in his high-pitched voice, his clipped Minnesota accent penetrating the sound of my footsteps.

"Oh, I'm doing pretty good, Virgil." I stopped and smiled up at his gaunt face.

I always enjoyed these small snippets of chatter with Virgil. We were fellow men of the soil after all, sharing an appreciation for the rudiments of agriculture, the long hours, the unforgiving weather, the ups and downs of the market. Most of the people I rubbed shoulders with in this park came from corporate America, retired executive types who had spent their lives behind a desk wearing a suit and tie. But Virgil and I, we were brothers.

"Well, what are you up to now?" Virgil asked, laying a gnarled hand on my shoulder. "Heading up to the clubhouse are you?"

"Yeah, I'm on my way to the library to check out a movie. What are you doing?"

He gestured toward the red rocks in front of his house. "Oh, I'm out looking for weeds, trying to keep ahead of them. You know how it goes."

"Oh yes, yes I do," I nodded my head, trying to look very concerned.

Virgil's weed weapon of choice was dangling from his hand. No puny little bottle of weed spray would suffice for him. Oh no. Virgil's very demeanor screamed "industrial strength" in all that he tackled. As he stared at his yard, he held a three-gallon tank from which a small hose coiled its way up to his hand. His long fingers were gripped around a large nozzle device that had a trigger. The very thought of entering a project under-equipped went against every fiber in Virgil's being.

"Yeah, it's a lot of work, you know, staying ahead of them weeds." He stood there in a dream-like state, gazing out at his red rock as if the place were covered with thick underbrush. But all I could see was red gravel covering every square inch of the ground. Not a green thing was anywhere in sight.

"How long you been out here, Virgil?"

"Oh, better part of an hour I guess, looking and waiting. Don't want to get one of them letters, you know."

"I see, I see. Yes, getting a letter would be bad."

"Oh no, don't want that." He chuckled and shook his head. "Just like farming, you know, gotta stay on top of things." He looked at me again and gave me a discerning nod.

"Oh yes, yes," I concurred solemnly. "Can't be too careful." We stood there for a moment in silence as we both looked down at his red rock.

"Ahem." I cleared my throat. "Well, I better be off now. Let you get back to work."

"Okay, you take care. Enjoy that movie. Say hi to Diana for me will you?" He smiled and waved.

"Okay, I will. See you later, Virgil." After I had walked a few yards down the street, I turned around and looked behind me. There he was, slowly walking over the red gravel, staring intently at the ground, nozzle pointed at the ready.

Suddenly, I felt very small. Virgil was hard at work, back on his farm again, toiling away under the noonday sun.

I was on my way to check out a movie.

Chapter 4

GETTING ACCLIMATED

The picture said it all.

He was a middle-aged man, thin-faced with a dark mustache. A blur of snowflakes swirled around his hooded head as he struggled mightily to scrape ice off the windshield of his car. In the background, I could see a blur of white against the backdrop of a distant stand of trees. But it was his face, a close-up of that contorted scowl that seemed to be screaming a thousand epithets against his fate that sent chills up my spine.

I looked up at the banner headline at the top of the page:

MAJOR BLIZZARD HITS PACIFIC NORTHWEST.

I shivered under my bathrobe.

It was early December. I had just awakened and was sprawled out in my recliner with my newspaper and my morning cup of coffee.

The weather for the day looked promising. A placid sunrise was already splashing over the surrounding mountains and flooding the East Valley with a gentle warmth. I remembered that last night on the news the weatherman had said it was going to get up into the mid-seventies today. I was ready for another beautiful day, another day of fun in the sun. But then, when I held the front page of the newspaper up to my eyes, the sight of that poor soul scraping his windshield during a blinding snowstorm slapped me in the face.

Suddenly, unexpectedly, a surge of guilt coursed through my body.

After all, despite the blizzard back home, I was still going to go spend the morning golfing with a friend, leisurely walking up and down the green grass of the fairways, relaxing under the warm Arizona sun. When I was through there, I was still going to take a dip in the pool and paddle around for a little bit, followed by a soak in the hot tub. I planned to top off my day by barbequing some steaks on the back patio and watching them sizzle to a perfect medium rare while downing a couple of beers under a gorgeous sunset.

Simply put, there would be no snowdrifts, no cold icy blasts, no shoveling of snow anywhere on my itinerary for the day.

Ah, but now, because of this pitiful picture, I knew that once in a while during the day, there was going to be a little something, somewhere in the back of my mind that would be reminding me: "Hey! Just because you're down here in seventy degree weather, walking around in T-shirts and shorts while your brethren back home are digging out of a blizzard, don't start thinking you're some mister big shot, because you're not. You're just warmer than they are, that's all."

I stared into space for a minute or two as I sorted through my feelings. Okay, so my friends and relatives back home are sliding around on icy roads, shoveling snow off their sidewalks, and pulling each other out of snowdrifts. There is nothing I can do about it a thousand miles away.

I put the paper down on the end table and sipped the last of my coffee. I will go about my day, I thought, but I will keep things in perspective, reminding myself often that I could be up there, too, struggling in the snow. I got up out of the chair to begin my day.

A short time later after I had showered and dressed, I walked into the kitchen. Diana was standing at the counter wearing her white bathrobe and busily buttering toast. "Hey, look what's happening back home," Diana said, waving a butter knife in the direction of the TV.

I turned and faced the screen in time to see a shot of a gloomy sight. A freeway was glazed over and headlights were stretching back forever. In the foreground, cars were off the side of the road and a couple of semis had jackknifed into the median. The reporter was saying that schools were closed and thousands of homes were without power.

"Yeah, I read about that in the paper," I replied.

I watched the TV as a couple of men pushed on the back of a car. Their breaths were swirling from their mouths as they strained against the back bumper with all their might. The car's wheels just spun uselessly on the ice.

I shuddered involuntarily at the sight and turned around, staring across the kitchen at the white door of the fridge. That's when I felt it for the first time. The TV had triggered it. Moving images had made more of an impact than the still picture in the newspaper. Was it possible to feel guilty and grateful at the same time? I had to suppress a smile. Then a laugh. It was all I could do to keep myself from jumping up out of my chair and shouting; "Hurray, I'm glad I'm not there!" But I thought better of it.

I took a bite of my toast, savoring the sweet taste of the strawberry jam. No, I wasn't going to say it to anyone, especially anyone back home. I wasn't going to rub it in their faces. But nonetheless, I was still glad I wasn't there.

And so I went about my day, lapping up the gorgeous scenery on the golf course, paddling around in the pool, and enjoying a luxurious soak in the hot tub, and polishing off those steaks later that evening.

It wasn't until I got a call from my sister later that night that I was reminded of the blizzard up north.

"Hey, have you been watching the news. We got dumped on." The excitement in her voice came through the phone loud and clear.

Uh oh, I thought, here it comes. Keep it in check now. "Uh, yeah, I've been watching that," I replied, trying to sound sympathetic. "Looks like you really had a good one blow through there."

"Yeah, roads were closed for a while. School was let out. It hasn't been much fun."

"I can imagine." With the phone to my ear, I grimaced and rubbed my forehead. Don't gloat, I said to myself. Don't rub it in. Be humble.

"So how are things down there? What did you do today?" she asked.

"Oh, well, not much. Tried to stay busy, you know. It's kinda boring down here."

"Really?"

"Oh yeah, yeah! Real boring."

"I thought there was always lots to do down there."

"Well…we have our days." Inwardly, I cringed. I was not enjoying this guilty feeling.

Mercifully, the conversation turned to nieces and nephews, how other members of the family were doing. We talked for several more minutes before I finally was able to hang up, thankful that no other mention of the weather was discussed.

As the weeks went by, I became more and more accustomed to my warm life under the sun. And while the guilty pangs became less intense with each picture I saw of people struggling in snowstorms, I still tried to keep things in perspective whenever I emailed or talked on the phone with friends and relatives back home.

The first month or so of living in Arizona always gives me a lot of opportunities to keep things in perspective. And so it was that an incident on a busy Mesa street after we had just arrived turned out to be another case in point.

After a shopping trip to Wal-Mart, I was sitting in my car at a stop sign, waiting to pull out of the parking lot. It was a long wait. I had been sitting there for five, ten, fifteen seconds, waiting for the stream of cars to go by. Waiting. Waiting, while my turn signal kept ticking away. When, all of a sudden I heard a honk behind me.

I was startled. I couldn't imagine why anyone would be honking at me. I was stuck at this stop sign for crying out loud. I couldn't go anywhere until this river of cars had passed by. Oh, I guess I could have peeled out and entered one of the tiny breaks in the traffic that came by from time to time. But it looked like it would be too risky, almost suicidal. I would just be inviting an accident, I thought. How could anyone squeeze into this traffic? I shrugged it off. The honk had to be accidental. Somebody must have leaned on their horn by mistake. I sat there calmly and waited for the traffic to abate.

Then there was a second honk.

The blood drained from my face. My eyes instinctively darted towards the rearview mirror. Sitting right behind me was the apparent source of the annoying honk, a bright red sports car. At the wheel sat a man of about thirty years of age, wearing tinted sunglasses that wrapped around his eyes. He was wearing a white sleeveless T-shirt and his blond hair was meticulously slicked back along the sides of his head. Muscles protruded from his sleeveless shirt like tree trunks, and his face was all scrunched up in a look of disgust. He resembled an angry Roman gladiator, sitting there with his jaw jutting out in defiance. When our eyes met in my rear-view mirror, he threw his hands up in the air, and his lips moved in a scathing, silent rant.

I could feel sweat starting to bead up on my forehead. I took a deep breath and stared back at the gladiator, his mouth silently spewing out a flood of obscenities. My hands gripped the steering wheel so tightly that my knuckles ached. I prayed for the traffic to hurry up and die down in front of me. Oh, please hurry! I don't want to die in a Wal-Mart parking lot.

Thankfully, the flow of cars ended. Breathing a sigh of relief, I eased out into the road, making a right turn with the image of the gladiator burning a hole in my brain. I couldn't wait to get back to the friendly and familiar confines of our retirement park.

Just then, my thoughts were interrupted by a roar coming up on my left. The shiny red sports car came up along side of me in a flash and instinctively I shot a glance in its direction.

There behind the wheel, with his right arm extended towards me as he gave me the universal single-finger sign of displeasure, sat Mr. Gladiator. The sun was glinting off of his dark glasses and his tan face was contorted in a show of rage. I barely had time to think about what I was seeing because, in an instant, he shot past me. I was left staring at the retreating trunk of his shiny red car.

I didn't know what to think. Don't let this bother you, I said to myself. He's the one with the problem, not you. Don't lose your patience. I smiled inwardly and prided myself at my calm demeanor in the face of adversity. I wasn't going to let some jerk set me off, get me mad, challenge me to a fight on the road. I had read about road rage incidents, and I wasn't about to get sucked into one.

Congratulating myself on my ability to stay composed, I

slowly began to apply the brakes on my car, as it approached a red light. Well done, I thought. I hadn't let some jerk bait me into an incident. I had held my cool, acted very civilized, kept my head. I was really starting to pat myself on the back, when suddenly my jaw dropped to my lap. I couldn't believe it. My car was rolling to a stop, right next to the same red sports car. Wonderful!

I felt myself begin to hyperventilate. Remain calm. Remain calm. He wasn't going to get out and come bash my head in. Was he? As my car came to a stop, I nonchalantly leaned my left elbow on the door and put my hand up to my forehead, shielding my eyes from his view with my fingers.

I tried to hum a tune to calm my nerves. Out of the corner of my eye, I could see the sun glinting off his shiny red car. It was so close I could have reached out and touched it if my window had been open. But I sat there staring straight ahead with my hand shielding my face, waiting for the light to turn green. I could hear the sound of idling engines, someone's stereo thumped a bass beat somewhere in the line of cars. Seconds dragged by slowly and I couldn't get my mind off of "him." I didn't know what he was doing, but I imagined the gladiator looking at me through those dark sunglasses, his eyes burning a hole through my hand, his face twisted in a hateful show of anger. Come on! Was this light ever going to turn green?

Finally, I couldn't stand it anymore. I had to peek at him. Like slowing down to look at a wreck, I had to see what he was doing. I stole a quick glance through my fingers. He was preoccupied with the knobs on his radio and seemingly oblivious to me, the source of his earlier rage.

I couldn't believe it. This guy was ready to rip me from limb to limb a half-minute ago, and now I was no longer of any interest to him? Oddly, I felt cheated. Deep in thought, I sat there for a moment staring down at the steering wheel.

Oh, I have to take another look, I said to myself. I have to make sure I saw what I saw. Again, I sneaked a peek through my fingers as they rested against the left side of my face. But the gladiator and his red sports car were gone.

It was then I heard the third honk of the day.

Not only was the gladiator gone, but everybody else was gone, too. I hadn't noticed that the light had changed and everybody was moving again. Everybody except me. Whoever it was that was sitting behind me honking, and I wasn't about to look back there this time, wanted me to move, and right now.

I immediately obliged, punching the gas pedal with my foot. Tires squealed and my head flew back against my seat. Geeze, I thought, as stores, restaurants, and parking lots zoomed by my window, people are sure in a hurry down here.

The next several weeks were spent in adjustment. And there was a big adjustment to make. Back home in rural Idaho, a stop sign was not looked at as an unwanted impediment in a daily commute; no, not at all. It was a place of peaceful repose. With no other cars around, sitting at a stop sign was a time to check cell phone messages or stare at the mountain ranges in the distance. And if a vehicle did happen to be coming down the adjacent road, my first inclination would not be to peel out of the intersection in front of him. My first thought would be to wait at the stop sign and see who it was. After all, we might know each other and want to wave.

A couple of weeks after the incident with the gladiator, I found myself sitting at the same stop sign, this time with Diana by my side. The familiar stream of vehicles cruised past in front of our car. I was fully used to this by now, the transformation completed days ago. No longer a dawdling nuisance crawling up and down the streets of Mesa, I had become one of them. I, too, was a frenetic motorist driving with wild abandon, looking for any opening I could squeeze into at a moment's notice.

Feeling the warmth of the sun on my left shoulder, I sat confidently at the wheel. The torrent of cars sped by in front of us as I watched impassively through the rearview mirror as a burgeoning procession lined up behind me.

I looked over at Diana. Seated in the passenger seat next to me, she was oblivious to the rush of traffic going past. With a tiny bottle of fingernail polish sitting in the armrest next to her, she was intently painting her fingernails. Her ever-present book was sitting at the ready on the dashboard in front of her.

My attention reverted back to the street in front of me. Down the road, I could see a small gap in the surging traffic and calmly assessed my situation. It wasn't much of an opening, but if timed right it would be enough to allow one or two vehicles to enter the street.

I poised my foot over the gas pedal and tightened my grip on the wheel as I awaited my chance. When it came, I acted with cool efficiency, as if it were as natural as taking a breath.

Punching the accelerator down to the floor, we roared away from the stop sign and turned sharply into the adjoining street. The book slid violently across the dashboard as if it had been shot out of a cannon and came to rest between my left leg and the door. Diana let out a guttural scream as her hands stabbed in the air to catch the fingernail polish bottle which had suddenly become a dangerous projectile. Our bodies were thrown about as if we were rag dolls as the car made a forceful ninety-degree turn onto the street.

I quickly sped up to merge in with the rest of the cars

and was soon driving with the flow of traffic. A perfectly timed maneuver, I thought. We would have been sitting there for days if not for my quick thinking. Then I looked over at Diana.

Her body was frozen in a pose that reminded me of a great athlete in action. She was twisted in an awkward position with her back resting against the door. Her hands were held above her head as she clasped the fingernail polish bottle with her fingers. She had a look of startled disbelief on her face. Her eyes were as big as saucers.

"Excuse me, but what the heck are you doing?" she yelled. "You could have gotten us killed."

Dumbfounded, I reached back into the deep recesses of my mind to come up with something to say. I blurted out the only thing I could think of. "I'm only driving," I said, shrugging my shoulders.

She continued to stare at me with big, uncomprehending eyes and the silence between us at that moment was deafening.

I could tell she wasn't buying any of it and I had to think of something fast. I took my right hand off the wheel and held it towards her palm up, as if pleading my case. With added emphasis on each syllable I continued, "Driving – in – Arizona."

∞

The picture said it all.

It was dawn somewhere up north. Two giant, yellow snowplows were climbing up a hill on a four-lane highway. A fountain of white snow was streaming from the front of their shiny blades and landing in a pile alongside the road. A line of cars with their headlights blazing through the early morning haze followed along behind. It looked like it was very cold.

I glanced at the story about another late winter storm hitting Utah and Idaho. Unconcerned, I skipped quickly to the sports page. Major league baseball teams were arriving in Arizona to prepare for the fast approaching spring training. I wanted to know the latest.

It was late February. I had just awakened and was sprawled out in my favorite chair with my newspaper and my morning cup of coffee.

The weather for the day looked promising. It was supposed to push up into the low eighties with plenty of sunshine. I had a full day planned. A trek in the desert with the hiking club would fill most of my day. I was looking forward to the breathtaking scenery, the formidable trail, and the camaraderie I enjoyed with my fellow hikers. The storm back home barely raised my interest.

During the last few months of my winter of warmth, I had become jaded. The self-consciousness and the humility I had possessed only a few months earlier were now gone. News of storms in other parts of the country was now met with a detached indifference. There was too much to do here in the sunshine to worry about, or even be aware of, what was going on elsewhere. Reports of winter weather in the north had become like a pesky mosquito buzzing around my head that I would absently swipe at with my hand, while I was busy with something else. It just wasn't that important anymore.

Later that night, I received the expected call from my sister back home. "Hey, you been watching the news? We got dumped on last night." Her voice had an edge to it, a sort of cabin fever quality.

"Oh, really? I'm sorry. I haven't been paying much attention."

"Yeah, roads were closed and school was let out again. It was a real mess. This has been one long winter, let me tell you."

"Gee, that's too bad. I guess I've been too busy to notice. Guess what the temperature was here today."

"What?"

"I think it got up to eighty-five."

"You lucky dog!"

As usual, the conversation turned to nieces and nephews, how other members of the family were doing. We talked for several more minutes, with me trying to find any opportunity to drop a hint or two about how warm it had been that day. My comments were jokingly met with sarcastic comebacks.

And so, the transformation was complete. As I hung up the phone I realized I had become a true Arizona snowbird, complete with an unsympathetic attitude towards my snowbound family back home. My comments to my sister had been purely in jest. Nevertheless, I still meant every word I had said. I was definitely glad to be where I was and I was no longer shy about saying so.

Yes, the transformation was complete indeed.

Chapter 5

THE INCIDENT AT
THE POST OFFICE

It was a warm December afternoon that day I saw her. She was standing unsteadily in the doorway of the post office, gazing out at the busy parking lot. The panicked confusion on her face seemed to contradict her state of impeccable dress.

The others and I stood there in line, holding our Christmas packages and holiday cards and watching her, wondering what she was going to do. The unusually warm sun bore down on us like we were pork ribs on a grill. Droplets of sweat began trickling down my neck underneath my shirt collar. The coolness of the doorway where she was standing up ahead, beckoned to me like an oasis in the desert.

She must have finished her business inside, because there was nothing in her hands but the straps of the red purse which was dangling by her right side. Yet, she just stood there immobilized, with a look of distress on her face.

The line at the post office, comprised mostly of old men, was naturally long that day. It was, after all, the Christmas season. No matter where you went in Mesa during that time of year, you could expect to wait in some sort of line. Restaurants, banks, checkout counters, it didn't seem to matter where you were. Everyone was out and about, doing their Christmas shopping and mailing.

The line started in front of the counter where the post office clerk stood and snaked out the front door and around the corner. It then stretched down the sidewalk alongside the front of the building.

I remained fixated on that woman. In the background, I could hear vehicles entering and leaving the parking lot. A whiff of exhaust would sometimes cause me to wrinkle my nose. People would get out of their cars and walk to the end of the line with a package in their hand. An occasional muffled cough could be heard. Those leaving the post office would hurriedly brush past the woman in the doorway on their way to their cars. Although she was inconveniently in the way, no one seemed to be bothered by her presence.

I slowly moved forward with the nameless faces in the line, studying the woman in the doorway. She was very thin and probably in her early eighties. The first thought I had when I saw her was that she looked peculiarly out of place. If she was just making a trip to the post office, the old woman was extremely overdressed.

She wore a stylish red dress with fashionable long sleeves and a pair of attractive matching dress shoes. Her dark hair had been expertly styled, and a long, shiny necklace was draped around her neck. The woman looked as if she belonged in the balcony at the ballet rather than in the doorway of a stuffy old post office. Whoever she was and whatever she was doing there that day, it was obvious she was used to the finer things in life.

The line inched forward. I shuffled my feet, holding my small parcel to my chest, feeling the sun bearing down on my bare head. I wiped my brow. Soon I got my first glimpse of her up close. And I was shocked at what I saw.

Her eyes gave it away immediately. Something was wrong. She stood in the doorway looking out at the parking lot while holding onto the doorframe for balance. Slowly, she looked from side to side apparently searching for something or someone.

As I got closer, I could see her lips moving as she mumbled something I couldn't hear. But it was her eyes, her terror-filled eyes, that stopped me in my tracks. There was no doubt this woman was scared out of her mind.

I'd seen that look before. Once, as a young boy growing up on our farm, I had chased a stray cat into the haystacks by the corrals. Cornering the poor animal, my eight-year-old mind had thought that it would be good sport to shoot it with my BB gun. With no way of escape, the cat hunched down next to the bales of hay and stared at me. As I stood there looking down the barrel of my BB gun into the cat's terror-stricken eyes, my self image of a rough, tough cowboy melted away, and I slowly lowered my gun, letting the cat slink away past my leg.

I saw that same look in this woman's eyes. The sight of them sent chills down my spine. This woman was in some kind of trouble. Someone should make an effort to assist her, I thought. Someone should ask her if she needed any help, let her know that someone cared, tell her that everything was going to be all right. What on earth was she doing here by herself?

I watched as the woman let go of the doorframe and began taking slow, unsteady steps away from the building. It was if she had finally decided to take the plunge, to leave the safety of the doorway and venture out into the unknown. The soles of her bright red shoes scraped along the sidewalk as she held her hands out to her side as if she were balancing on a surfboard. She held her head straight, staring straight ahead with her panicked-looking eyes. The red purse in her right hand swayed with each uneasy shuffle.

Instantly, those of us waiting in line became an audience of a great drama. As we stood there silently clutching our packages, our focus shifted. We had become a united group of strangers, our focus now drawn to the woman and her predicament, whatever it was. The possibilities of what would happen next connected all of us together in a state of suspense. Suddenly, the reason for which we were all there in the first place, to mail Christmas packages, had become secondary.

I watched as the woman shuffled slowly and unsteadily towards the curb. Stepping away from the shade of the doorway for the first time, her red dress dazzled brilliantly in the bright afternoon sun. Everyone in line was following her every move. She stopped when she reached the edge of the sidewalk, teetering there for a moment on top of the curb, contemplating her next course of action.

She looked down at the curb, still holding her arms out to her side for balance, her red purse swinging back and forth. She tentatively lifted her right foot and lowered it a couple of inches down the side of the curb. She looked like she was dipping her toes in the cool water of a mountain lake. This lasted only a second or two, as she began to tilt a little to one side and a soft "oh" escaped from her lips. She quickly set her foot back down again on the solid cement beneath her feet.

Looking up, she gazed out into the parking lot once again, teetering on the edge of the curb. Although it was only six or eight inches to the pavement below her feet, to this woman on this day, she might as well have been standing at the edge of the Grand Canyon.

We all stood there breathlessly watching the drama unfold. Nobody said a word. Nobody moved. Time was frozen.

Again, I wondered why she was standing there alone. Somebody should help her, I thought. Surely there must be someone here who knows her. She couldn't have driven here by herself. If anyone was looking for an opportunity in their day to be a Good Samaritan, this was it. Why wasn't anyone helping her? More to the point, why wasn't I helping her?

It only seemed natural that somebody should be stepping forward to give her a hand. But for the longest time, no one moved, including me.

A few moments later, the old lady made another attempt at stepping off the sidewalk, gingerly lowering her foot down to the pavement. My brain began sending signals to my arms and legs. Get moving you idiot. Set the package down and go help her.

But I didn't even get a chance to move a muscle. Out of the corner of my eye, I saw somebody hurrying towards her. Somebody had beaten me to it. And when I saw who it was, I was utterly stunned.

After standing in line for the better part of the last fifteen minutes, I had assumed that everyone behind me was just like me – slow, gray-haired, wrinkled, and over fifty-five, (a buzzword in Arizona, especially in the winter). Those were the only people I'd seen getting out of their cars and walking to the back of the line. There must have been thousands of us so-called "senior citizens" living within a square mile of the post office.

But the person who was walking over to help the woman was not one of us. Not at all. In fact, she couldn't have been more different.

She was young, very young, twenty-two or twenty-three, with short blonde hair that gleamed in the afternoon sun as she walked by. She had on a very short pair of shorts that showed off her long tan legs, which were accentuated by her bare feet, bright red toenails, and blue flip-flops. Her matching blue tank top exposed a slim, attractive midriff and my nostrils detected a hint of exotic perfume as she walked by. Oh no. She wasn't one of us at all. She could have walked out of the pages of a glamour magazine.

Where she came from, I did not know; but it had to have been from somewhere in the line behind me. I never noticed her there before. But her sudden appearance perked up the audience of old men to say the least.

We all watched spellbound as the young woman hurried over to the lady on the curb. She set her package down on the sidewalk, and gently put her left arm around the woman's shoulder.

"Are you looking for your car?" she asked in a soft, reassuring voice. "Can I help you find your car?"

The old lady, still standing on the edge of the curb, looked up at the young woman, her first acknowledgement of someone else's presence. Standing in the line not more than ten feet away, I could see that the old woman's eyes were still filled with terror.

Nothing was said between them for several seconds. Both of them just stood there on the top of the curb looking into each other's faces. The old woman looked as if she was confused, and was probably trying to figure out who this stranger was that had suddenly appeared at her side. The young woman continued to smile at her, trying to look reassuring.

"Are you looking for your car?" The young woman asked again. "Should we go out here and try to find your car?" This time she gently nudged the old woman forward, trying to coax her to step off the curb.

With her left arm gently wrapped around the old lady's

shoulders and her other hand holding onto the older woman's hand, together they slowly stepped off of the curb.

The people in line were mesmerized now, our parcels, our lists of errands, our busy days long forgotten. A few minutes ago, we were all holding our packages, impatient with the wait, wishing the line would move just a little bit faster. But now, we wished we didn't have to move forward at all.

They walked a few steps away from the curb and then stopped. "Do you think your car's out here?" the young woman asked, still holding on to the older woman, her arm wrapped around her shoulder.

Gaps were forming in the line. It was becoming a huge annoyance now to have to move forward and risk missing out on the show. "Next" the voice of the clerk inside could be heard periodically saying. We dreaded hearing that word now. Nothing seemed more important than following the plight of this poor woman, who was now seemingly safe in the arms of her rescuer.

The old lady hesitated for a moment, gazing out into the near full parking lot. Then she slowly turned and looked into the young woman's face. "Yes, yes," she replied in a raspy voice.

"Okay, you think your car's out here? Which one do you think it might be?" They stood there looking at the sea of cars in front of them. The young blonde let go of the older woman's hand. "Do you see your car anywhere around here?"

The old woman stood there motionless and uncertain. The young woman exhibited extreme patience, letting the old lady take her time, looking at first one car, then another.

She seemed more confused than ever now. The old woman's head moved from side to side as if searching for something familiar, a color, a style, anything that might trigger a spark of memory into her mind. The young blonde continued to stand at her side patiently, her arm still wrapped around the older woman's shoulder.

"How about over here?" the young woman asked as she slowly turned the old woman around to her right, facing the cars that were parked directly in front of the building, their front tires butting up against the curb. "Do you see your car over here somewhere?"

I tore my eyes away from the drama before me and glanced down the line. Everyone's eyes were fixed on the two women standing in the parking lot. An older man with both arms wrapped around a large rectangular package, chose that exact moment to lift his head and look in my direction. Our eyes locked for an uncomfortable few seconds before we both hurriedly looked away. While this was something we were all witnessing together, we preferred to perceive it privately and quietly within the confines of our own thoughts.

The old woman peered intently at the first car in the row in front of her. A dark red sedan sat empty just in front of them. The car was no more than ten feet away, an older model that was beginning to show its age.

The old woman stood there for a second. Then her eyes suddenly widened and a flash of recognition crossed her face. "Yes, yes," she said in her raspy voice, slowly raising her arm and pointing a long, bony finger at the car.

"Is that your car?" the young woman asked.

"Yes, yes," the old lady repeated, now nodding her head vigorously as she pointed at the car.

"All right, let's go over there okay? Can you make it over there?

"Yes, yes," the old woman repeated again. For the first time there was hope in her eyes.

Together, they walked slowly over to the car. The young

blonde patiently guided the old lady forward, reassuringly holding onto her hand, while resting her other hand gently on the older woman's back.

Those of us in line stood still as stone statues watching the two women.

This was crazy, I thought. The prospect of this woman driving herself to the post office was no more plausible than the thought of me jumping off of Niagara Falls. What was she going to do, get behind the wheel and peel away, suddenly transformed from the fragile, confused being that was walking in front of us to a competent, alert motorist? The idea was laughable and scary at the same time.

As the two of them got closer to the car, the old lady headed for the passenger's door on the right side of the empty vehicle. She reached for the shiny chrome door handle, wrapping her wrinkled hand around it, and giving it a weak tug. The door wouldn't budge. She pulled again, this time leaning backwards with her body and jerking her arm a couple of times, trying to force the door open. Still no response.

"Are you sure this is your car?" the young blonde asked gently. "It seems to be locked and there's nobody inside."

The old woman acted as though she hadn't heard her. She summoned up all of her strength, feeble as it was, and leaned back with everything she had, jerking frantically against the shiny handle. The door did not yield. The old woman's hand fell limply to her side.

"It's not going to open, honey," the young woman said. She grabbed the handle and pulled on it. "See? It's locked."

The terror in the old woman's eyes returned. She dropped her head dejectedly and put her hand to her forehead, confused, bewildered, scared.

"Don't worry. We'll find your car," the young blonde said with a reassuring smile, trying to inject a note of optimism into the situation. "Maybe it's over here. Could it be over on this side?" Slowly, she turned the old woman around.

Instinctively, those of us in line turned our heads to the left. Twenty feet in front of the two women was yet another line of cars parked next to the curb.

This could take all day I thought. With the parking lot nearly full, it seemed as if locating this woman's car was going to be like finding a needle in a haystack. Were they going to go from car to car until they found one that wasn't locked? This was crazy!

The old woman squinted her eyes and peered intently in front of her. She stood there silently for a long time, the young blonde standing next to her with an arm soothingly resting on the old woman's back. Gradually, a crooked finger was raised in the direction of the first car.

"Do you think that's your car?"

The old woman took a few halting steps towards it and stopped to focus once again. Slowly, she started nodding.

"Is that it?" the young woman asked softly, showing admirable patience.

"Yes, yes," the old woman croaked, excitedly nodding her head and pointing.

"All right honey, let's go check it out okay?"

"Yes, yes."

And so like a slow motion tennis match, our heads slowly turned once again as the two woman set off in the direction of the car. We watched silently as they crept along in front of us, heading back in the direction from which they started. The young blonde showed no signs of irritation, cheerfully and gently guiding the old woman along.

The car they were walking towards was a fairly new, dark red Ford Ltd. with Arizona license plates. Behind the steering wheel was a newspaper lifted up high, obscuring the face of someone sitting in the driver's seat. Old, gnarled hands could be seen clutching the edges of the paper.

Slowly but surely, the two women made their way to the car with a deliberate and measured pace. All eyes were on them as they inched their way around the trunk and marched resolutely along the passenger's side to the front door.

Would this be the one? Would the poor woman finally find her car? This really didn't seem like a logical choice because whoever was sitting in the driver's seat didn't seem to be concerned at all about the possibility of having a confused passenger wandering about in the parking lot. The newspaper hadn't moved an inch.

At last the two women arrived at their destination. The old woman reached for the door handle, gave it a pull and the door opened a crack. Instantly, the newspaper behind the steering wheel came down like a shot, revealing the face of an old, wrinkled man who was smartly dressed and well groomed. He glanced at the elderly woman and then his right hand reached down for the ignition. The car's engine started with a roar.

The young woman helped open the car door for the old lady and guided her into the seat. With a smiling face, she said something to the older woman which could not be heard over the running engine and gently patted her shoulder. She stepped back and closed the door, making sure it was secure.

We all watched incredulously as the old man in the car slowly backed out of the parking place and drove off, leaving the young woman standing there in the sun.

She remained there watching the car stop at a stop sign before it slowly entered the adjoining street. Then she smiled and started walking back to the sidewalk where she retrieved her package. A chorus of nervous coughs and the clearing of throats could be heard as those of us in line tried to get back to the business at hand.

When the young woman stepped back up onto the sidewalk, the crowd silently parted like the Red Sea and she resumed her spot in the line.

A few minutes later, I was standing in front of the clerk inside the building. As he handed me my change for the Christmas package I was sending to my aunt back in Maryland, he paused and looked at me with a quizzical expression.

"What was all that fuss about outside?" he asked, holding my change in midair.

I opened my mouth, thinking for a moment that I wasn't going to get my money until I answered. But suddenly I realized I had no idea where to begin.

Did I want to try and explain to him that there was this old woman, who probably should not have even been allowed out of her house by herself, lost in the parking lot of his post office? Did I even want to try and tell him about the blonde bombshell (whom he would see in a minute) who came to the rescue of this older woman and helped her find her car?

And how could I describe to him the old woman's husband, if that's who he was, and how he didn't even seem to be concerned about her? The only way I could even conceive of such behavior was that he must have been in worse shape than she was. I shuddered at the thought.

Instead, I simply shrugged my shoulders. "Oh, nothing much, somebody was just helping a woman find her car."

The clerk looked at me and grunted absently. He dropped my change into the palm of my hand and I turned around to leave. On my way out, I sneaked one last peek at the star of the afternoon, the young, buxom blonde who was standing in line a few places behind me.

Blood rushed through my veins and my mind raced. Should I dare look forward to the day when I can't find my car? I hadn't even gotten out of the building before the answer came crashing back, a resounding *probably not*!

Chapter 6

THE BINGO DRAMA UNFOLDS

Bingo night! Whether some strange woman offered to rub you with her pig or not, bingo night each Wednesday was like no other night of the week, especially in my snowbird world.

Every Wednesday night, the ballroom was always packed with a couple of hundred bingo hopefuls. There's a joyous optimism in the air as we all sit there waiting for the night's festivities to begin.

On this particular bingo night in January, the majority of the crowd had been there for the better part of an hour, idling the time away in various pursuits such as reading, playing cards, or visiting with one another. Some took great pride in lining up their arsenal of bingo daubers on the table in front of them, inspecting their readiness for the big night.

Bingo was a huge event for the winter resort community in which we lived. Seating was always at a premium, so arriving early was an absolute must if you wanted a good seat. Actually, it had become my observation that retired folks in Arizona arrived close to one hour early for everything, everywhere. So this "early arrival" ritual wasn't exactly limited to bingo.

So many times I'd made that trek up to the clubhouse for

the big night. And each new week, I would make that short, ten-minute walk with renewed enthusiasm and a quickened step. As I would open the door and enter the building, I felt as if all the disappointment, all the discouragement and all the heartache from past bingo nights would be wiped clean from the slate. I would buy my bingo cards and take my seat with the self-assuredness that tonight would be my night.

Ah, yes…bingo night! Why, I couldn't imagine a Wednesday night in Arizona without it.

But it hadn't always been that way.

When Diana and I first arrived in Arizona for our winter's visit from our potato farm in Idaho, bingo was barely a blip on our radar screen. It was on the periphery, just one of dozens of activities vying for our attention. But as time went on, I slowly started to get the feeling that just maybe, I was missing out on something. On Wednesday nights, cars were parked all up and down the street in front of the clubhouse like no other night of the week. The place swarmed with people. Bingo's grip on the retired populace was hard to ignore.

Soon bingo had become a subliminal message blaring at me from the din of everyday life. As I would drive down the streets of Mesa, jockeying for position in the impatient traffic, supermarkets, banks, and restaurants would flip endlessly by, giving way every block or so to the retirement communities with bingo signs out by the front gates. Why, I would catch the word "Bingo" darting past, out of the corner of my eye for what seemed like a couple hundred times a week.

Finally, one Wednesday night, I couldn't stand it any longer. What was all this fuss about? I just had to go find out.

"There you go," the woman named Mary said as she handed the dauber back to me. "You are officially rubbed tonight by the lucky pig." She had "graciously" shared the luck of her pig by rubbing it up and down my dauber, the ink-filled cylindrical tube used to mark the bingo sheets. She sat back in her chair with an air of self-confidence as if she had just bestowed on me a valuable gift.

Just then a loud, booming male voice almost jolted us out of our chairs. Its deep inflections reverberated throughout the large ballroom like a peal of thunder.

"Ladies and gentlemen, I would like to welcome each and every one of you to bingo night."

In an instant, the big ballroom, previously loud with conversation, fell as silent as a tomb. Everyone stopped what they were doing and sat up in their chairs. The bingo caller, a thin man with dark hair, who up to this point had been sitting quietly on the stage up front, quickly took command of the room.

"There are a few rules we should go over before we can begin." He held sway over the audience as his monotone voice continued.

The huge crowd sat quietly as the caller's deep voice droned on, ticking off the rules. When he finally finished, he ended on a hopeful note. "Good luck to one and all."

He flicked on a switch and the soft whirring of the bingo machine permeated the room as the numbered ping-pong balls tumbled around inside a clear plastic bubble next to his table. The sound of chairs scraping across the floor could be heard as some in the crowd scooted up closer to their tables. All conversation came to a halt as everyone's concentration suddenly focused on the task at hand. I looked up and down our table. Hands rose with bingo daubers poised resolutely over their bingo cards. Heads were bowed as all eyes focused on the dizzying column of numbers lying there in front of them.

Then as if God were speaking to Moses from the

mountaintop, the bingo caller's booming voice began the slow cadence of numbers with the first number of the night.

"b eleven."

The crowd silently pored over the numbered boxes. My right hand, with the pig-anointed dauber gripped firmly in my fingers, scrolled rapidly up and down the six bingo cards on the table in front of me. It seemed like an instant, a mere flash of time, but just as I finished checking out the last column and determined that there were no "b-11's" to mark, the caller announced the next number.

"g fifty-four."

I glanced quickly across the table at Mary and her friend Dorothy. No longer concerned with me, their determined faces intensely scanned their bingo games. Mary bit her lower lip in concentration. Dorothy's expression was one of sheer focus as she expertly examined her numbered boxes with a wave of her dauber.

"o sixty-five."

Amid the soft whirring of the bingo machine, the mono-tone voice forcefully boomed number after number through the thick silence of the ballroom. Our heads were lowered like sheep grazing in a pasture as we raked our eyes over the jumble of numbers spread out before us. I struggled to reach the last number on my page before the imposing voice announced the next number.

"i twenty."

I stole a glance across the table. Mary and Dorothy seemed to be in agony. Both frowned and slowly shook their heads as they stared down at their numbers. Apparently it wasn't going their way.

"o seventy."

On it went. The succession of numbers boomed over the crowd in numbing repetition. My bingo card filled up rapidly and just when I thought I might have a chance at winning this game, my worst fears came to pass.

"B four."

A woman on the other side of the room excitedly screamed "BINGO" as if she had suddenly noticed the place was ablaze and she was screaming "Fire!" Instantly, the crowd let out a loud and dejected groan and the room filled with rising voices.

"I needed just two more numbers," Mary said, shaking her head in disgust. Her dauber remained poised over her bingo game.

"I wasn't even close," Dorothy snarled, while violently snatching up the used bingo page and wadding it up into a ball.

The loss was disappointing. Dejectedly, I discarded my used bingo page in the plastic bag taped at the edge of the table and got ready for the next game. Aside from winning, the best part about playing bingo was the fact that you didn't really have time to feel sorry for yourself. The next game started immediately and any depression you might have had from losing was quickly extinguished by the hope – yes there was always hope – of winning the next game.

And so it went, game after game, number after number. Like a predictable script, the night flowed with unerring certainty; the precise cadence of the bingo caller slicing through the stifling silence of the crowd, the constant whirring of the bingo machine in the background, and the dreaded but expected "BINGO" yelled from somewhere in the room, followed by the loud, miserable groan. And then the slowly rising hope of the next game.

Minutes turned into an hour, then two hours. Soon we finished the ninth game, the next to the last game of the night, and no one at our table had won a thing.

"Well, that does it," Mary sighed as she sat back in her

chair and took a deep breath. "If we're not lucky on the coverall, then my pig will have come up empty again."

I looked down next to Mary's bingo daubers. There, lying forlornly on its side was the small, pink stuffed pig. I wondered if it realized just how much of a failure it had been so far tonight. "Maybe you should rub our daubers again with your pig," I said, nodding to the little creature. "We might need another dose of luck."

"Oh no, no," said Mary wagging her finger at me and shaking her head. "Only once a night and only before the games begin." The words rolled off her tongue as if she had said them many times before. "Otherwise, it would bring bad luck, not good luck."

"Maybe you should put the danged pig in your purse and forget the whole thing," said Dorothy sarcastically, shooting an approving glance in my direction. Mary turned towards her friend with the force of a bobcat jumping out of a tree. "Dorothy, you know perfectly well that I…"

"Ladies and gentlemen, I would like to thank each and every one of you for coming out tonight."

The stentorian voice pierced the room like a missile flying through the air. Mary and Dorothy looked towards the front of the crowded ballroom.

"The last game of the night is the progressive coverall. Every number must be covered before a bingo can be declared."

Mary and Dorothy settled back in their chairs and reached for their daubers, their little spat quickly forgotten. Nothing could get in the way of the coverall. The crowd sat quietly, daubers in hand, as the caller continued with his final pronouncement of the evening.

"If you bingo on or before tonight's progressive number, you will win one thousand dollars. Once the progressive number is passed, the pot will be worth one hundred dollars. Tonight's progressive number is fifty-six. I wish each and every one of you good luck."

I should be able to "Bingo" before the fifty-sixth number is called, I thought to myself. I allowed my brain to conjure up a myriad of things I could buy with a thousand dollars, things like golf clubs, new clothes, meals in fancy restaurants. I had been watching this number rise over the last few weeks, fifty-three, fifty-four, fifty-five. In my mind, tonight was the night that it was certainly going to go.

Progressive coverall bingo was what kept us coming back. It preyed on the little bit of greed in each of us and gave us usually tightfisted senior citizens a huge financial incentive to plunk our money down on a few bingo games.

There were seventy-five numbers in bingo. The progressive number started at forty-nine and rose by one each week until someone covered all their spaces on, or before the night's progressive number (the number of numbers called). Each week, the chances of a big winner being in our midst would increase.

The caller announced the first number in the coverall.

"B twelve."

As the minutes wore on, the spaces on my card filled up, and I could feel that familiar tugging of the heart, the feeling of cautious optimism rising up within me.

"G fifty-five"

I glanced over at Mary and Dorothy. They remained focused, intent. With daubers in hand, they scrolled up and down each column very deliberately, occasionally plastering an uncovered space with ink. I don't think they'd have noticed if a hurricane had blown through the ballroom.

Number after number was called until incredibly I had only two more numbers to go. I gave the electronic bingo board up on the wall a quick look. Fifty-four numbers had been called. I was agonizingly close to winning the big one.

"o sixty-three."

There was one of them. I slammed the head of my dauber down on the uncovered space. Orange ink splattered every-where. I looked down at my card and saw a slathering of orange covering every space but one. There, in the N column, peeking up at me as if it were a lost soul peering out from the depths of an orange abyss was the uncovered and pristine number thirty-four. My heart leaped up in my throat. N thirty-four! That was all that was standing between me and the Promised Land.

I looked out over the crowd. You could cut the tension with a knife. Everyone had their eyes riveted on their bingo cards with their daubers held out in front of them. How many were as close as I was? Images of what I could buy with my winnings once again danced in my head.

I looked across the table at Dorothy and Mary. They were staring at their cards with frowns on their faces. "I have only one more number to go," I whispered.

They quickly peeked at my bingo card and then shot me a supportive glance. Mary smiled and held up a pair of crossed fingers. Again, the bingo caller's booming voice pierced the thick silence.

"Ladies and gentlemen, the next number I call will be the fifty-sixth number of the coverall game. If no bingo is called on the next number, the pot drops from one thousand dollars to one hundred dollars, and we will continue until we get a winner. Good luck."

I watched nervously as the caller reached down and picked up the ping-pong ball. He looked at it for a moment and then at all of us sitting there waiting. I stared down at my card. My hand trembled as I held the dauber over "N thirty-four." I suddenly became aware of my terribly dry throat and tried to swallow. As I gulped, my eyes remained riveted on the only empty square on my card. It seemed like an eternity before the booming voice broke the stifling silence.

"I nineteen."

Instantly, a soft squeaky voice from two tables over piped up. "BINGO!"

A tremendous groan rose up from the frustrated throng, followed immediately by a rising sound of excited voices and the general pushing back of chairs.

I sat dumbfounded at the table, feeling as though I had just taken a huge body blow. I found myself gasping for air.

"Oh, what a shame," Mary exclaimed as both women got up and began putting on their coats. "You had just one more number. That's so sad."

"I thought I had it won," I mumbled, the dauber still in my hand, poised over the page. I sat perfectly still amid all the bustle around me, trying to comprehend what had just happened.

"Well, we better be off now." Mary waved goodbye, apparently not willing to commiserate with me in my time of pain. "Maybe we'll see you here again next week."

I remained seated and waved at them weakly, watching as they melted into the exiting throng.

I looked in front of me two tables over and there, appearing sporadically behind the departing bingo players, was the object of my pain, the man who yelled bingo. You could tell he was the winner a mile away. He sat at his table with a huge grin on his face, looking up at the occasional well-wisher who came to offer congratulations and a pat on the back.

Although we had never been formally introduced, I recognized him as someone I'd often seen around our park. I wasn't sure, but I thought his name might have been Fred. At any rate, he now had *my* thousand dollars.

I finally stood up and put on my coat. It was a cool evening and the fresh air felt good against my face as I walked back to the house. I would try to forget this, I told myself. After all, next week there would be another chance to win.

The following few days were a time of mourning. Moving on was not easy. I was constantly reminded of my pain whenever I saw "him" again. And I saw "him" often, at the post office, at the library, at the pool. There he would be, smiling away, enjoying his life, completely unaware of the pain he had caused me.

Oh, he wasn't just some innocent guy named Fred anymore. Oh no. To me, he would forevermore be the guy who yelled bingo, the guy who snatched a thousand dollars right out of my hand.

It turned out to be a long week before the next bingo night and another chance at redemption.

Chapter 7

A SLICE OF GOLF

The blue tee pushed through the soft, damp earth of tee box number one like a hot knife slicing through butter. While bending over, I released the golf ball and gently lifted my hand. The white, dimpled ball remained perfectly still, balanced on top of the tee, two or three inches above the ground. I stood up slowly and took a deep breath.

This is it, I thought, the moment of truth.

Three strangers stood behind me, quietly leaning on their golf clubs; men I had just met a few minutes earlier. Having just finished their drives off the tee, they were now my audience, front row spectators, too. I looked down the length of the fairway. The bright green grass sprawled out in front of me like a carpet that had just been unfurled. While the par five was generously wide with ample room to direct a shot, I still had my trepidations. It had been six months since I'd last swung a club. Where this ball would go was anybody's guess.

To make matters worse, the three men behind me were not the only ones watching me. Behind them, waiting for their turn to tee off, were four other foursomes of men, all strangers to me. Some were sitting in their carts and talking softly to each other. Others were quietly taking practice swings with determined looks of concentration in their eyes.

All would witness my first swing, good or bad. The saying, "you never get a second chance to make a first impression" could never have been more aptly applied.

It was a beautiful morning and my first day as a member of this men's golf league, a group from our park that I had decided to join on a whim. The red Superstition Mountains in the east framed against the bright blue cloudless sky towered over the golf course. A cool, comfortable breeze wafted over us from the west, cool enough to prompt many of us to don jackets as we began our rounds. Occasionally, the distant caw of a crow would punctuate the still, morning air. It was the perfect morning, the kind of morning that made you feel lucky to be alive. If all I had to do was just stand there and look, I would have been happy, content to take it all in. But I had to hit the ball. Everyone was waiting.

Golf had never been my passion, just an occasional pastime. Whenever I stood at the first tee of any golf course, one question would always run through my mind: why is this game so complicated? Getting my head around it seemed simple enough. Swing club, hit ball. Nothing real difficult. But through all the years of shanked shots, missed putts, lost balls, and high scores, one constant always prevailed. Golf was a great enigma to me.

There was the challenge of it, the pull of it, something that always made me want to return and give it another try. Oh, I had walked off many an eighteenth green cursing that I would never be back. (And I had witnesses to prove it, too.) But I always did come back – willingly, a glutton for punishment.

I held my first golf club as a boy of about six or seven. My mother, of all people, introduced me to the game, which happened quite out of the blue one summer's day. "Come on, get in the car," she'd said as she folded the last towel in the stack. "We're going golfing." Wiping her brow with the back of her hand, she carried the towels to the bathroom.

"What?" I said, interrupting my spit-spraying motor sounds as I halted my dump truck along the floor of our living room. Sitting up in my little bib overalls, I watched her retreat down the hall. "What's golfing?" I asked of nobody in particular.

She heard me.

"It's a game," she said as she came back out of the bathroom empty-handed. Her soft, oval face seemed permanently marked by that furrowed brow which gave the impression that my mother was always worrying about something. "It's time we got out of this house for a while." There was a spring in her step that I had seldom seen as she walked back down the hall towards me. When she reached the front door, she grabbed her purse and turned to face me. "Come, get in the car."

I was too young to appreciate it then, but she must have been dreadfully bored sitting in that house out in the country all summer long. Golfing would be something new, something different, an adventure of my mother's own choosing. After all, the role of a farmer's wife in those days did not carry with it the most independent of feelings.

As there was no golf course in Aberdeen back then, we had to drive the thirteen miles to American Falls on that sunny June day to go golfing. It was the beginning of twice weekly excursions with my mom that were a lot of fun.

We were never very good, hacking at the ball and more often than not, missing it all together. And walking the course was a killer, since it was rather hilly and golf carts were unheard of back then. But it was the time I spent with my mom that was so special, walking the fairways, talking, laughing, being out of the house and doing something together that nobody else was doing but us. It wasn't just fun. It was something that, well, just made me feel good.

All that came to an abrupt end late one afternoon on a hot, cloudy August day. We had just finished with the first hole and were halfway down the second fairway when the sky opened up, and we both started getting drenched.

"Damn it!" my mom yelled, looking up at the sky as if this happened only because we were there. "Come on, let's get out of here." She grabbed me by the hand and we started running for the clubhouse, pulling our rented set of golf clubs behind us. At one point, my mother slipped on the wet grass and fell, rolling halfway down a hill, spilling the contents of her golf bag all over the grass.

"Damn it, damn it, damn it!" she screamed as she bent over and began collecting the clubs. All the while sheets of rain assailed us from above.

The drive home was quiet. We were both soaked and cold. Water dripped from our hair. The smell of wet clothes permeated the inside of the car. My mother stared straight ahead with her hands firmly on the steering wheel, not saying a word, the windshield wipers flipping back and forth in constant rhythm. I could tell by the look on her face that she was angry. I dared not say anything, so I sat quietly in the passenger seat all the way home.

That would be the last time I went golfing with my mom. We never went back. There were times later on that I longed to go again. But she never offered and remembering how mad she got the last time we went, I never brought it up. As far as I can recall, she never took the sport up again at any other point in her life. But those few weeks of golfing with my mom introduced me to a sport I would dabble in for years to come.

I straightened my back, spread my feet slightly apart,

and pointed my toes in the direction of the ball. I closed my eyes for a second, and tried to relax and breathe in deeply. The muffled voices of the men behind me died down as I gently set the black, bulbous head of my Big Bertha driver next to the golf ball atop the blue tee.

All was quiet. I turned and looked down the length of the fairway one last time. This was going to be tricky, I thought. Bordering both sides of the grass on hole number one – and on most of the other holes, as I would find out later – was a huge area of wild desert. Thick, rolling brush and tall saguaro cacti were scattered throughout this area. If my ball didn't sail down the fairway and bounce happily on the grass that was stretched out in front of me, it would be gobbled up by a godforsaken wilderness that was fit for neither man nor beast. With the eyes of my new friends as an unwanted audience boring in on me, I could see a nightmare scenario in the making.

I quickly ran through a mental checklist of everything I thought important. Head down. Keep my eyes on the ball. Knees slightly bent. Keep my eyes on the ball. Feet equally spread. Keep my eyes on the ball. Slow, easy back swing. Keep my eyes on the ball. Rotate hips. Keep my eyes on the ball. Nice easy follow-through.

I tried to picture the perfect swing. But the sight of my ball slicing off into the wilds of the Serengeti kept emerging into my head.

Oh yes, the slice. I forgot to tell you. In the handful of times when I would hit the links back home during the summer, a huge banana-like slice had become my constant companion on my drive off the tee. I had succumbed to trying all sorts of mechanical gyrations to try and get rid of it, most of them proposed by my brother who was an avid and accomplished golfer. But no matter what I did, I would usually be greeted with the sight of my ball curling off to the right, while I stood there at the tee box frozen in my follow-through.

After that day in the rain with my mother, I never golfed much again as a boy. Later as a young adult, I would occasionally go out with a group of friends for a social round or two, but nothing really competitive. Just a nice friendly game of golf with the guys.

It wasn't until I was in my thirties that the game started really pulling me back into its fold. Aberdeen had just built a brand new, nine-hole golf course, and it had quickly become the talk of the town. Everyone was running out there to hit a few balls. Soon, it became painfully apparent by the tone and tenor at the town's only coffee shop, that if you weren't golfing, you were now some sort of new misfit who had nothing useful to contribute to the general discourse of the community. So for the first time in my life, I bought a set of clubs and diligently began playing golf at least once a week.

It was hard, hacking at the ball, willing it to go straight, chipping across to the other side of the green, and putting the ball way past the cup. But by the end of that summer, I had reined in most of my bizarre blunders to the point of a vague manageability. I was finally golfing what I considered to be a respectable game, with scores in the mid-fifties. But the slice. Oh, that slice was always popping up.

My brother Mike, on the other hand, took to the game like a duck takes to water. While I struggled hole after hole after inexorable hole, Mike steadily took on the qualities of a golfing whiz, leaving me in the dust and surpassing me in both skill and judgment. Our games together, competitive at first, eventually became a woeful exhibition between the have and the have-not.

"Maybe you should stand a little closer to the ball," he

would say patiently, as I stood there in my post-swing pose watching the ball drift off to the right and land in the next fairway. This, after he had just hit his ball straight ahead, splitting the fairway in two, watching it bounce as if it were a laser-guided missile on a path straight for the pin.

Whenever I did happen to hit my drive straight down the fairway, Mike would excitedly yell from behind me. "There you go. That's a good one. Now swing like that every time and you'll be fine."

Sadly, when we were climbing back into the cart, I would have to tell him that I had no way of knowing what it was that I had done differently on that swing than on any of the thousands of other golf swings that I had taken in my life.

Eventually, my game settled into a predictable pattern of semi-mediocrity with occasional flashes of brilliance.

As the years went by and golfing began to take more and more of a back seat while other interests moved in to take its place, I soon found myself on the golf course only a handful of times a year.

That was why I hesitated when I read in our park's news-letter one day shortly after arriving in Arizona:

GOLF AND MORE GOLF, MEN'S 18-HOLE GOLF LEAGUE
For more information, call Art

It sounded like fun. I needed something to jump start my snowbird routine. Don't get me wrong. Life in Arizona was great. No snow. No blizzards. No icy roads. But after a while, you have to start doing something, anything, or you will go crazy. Just sitting around being glad you're not in the snow can only take you so far.

There was only one problem though. As a golfer, I sucked.

Oh, I had golfed occasionally with a friend or two here and there since coming to Arizona, but joining a league would be a different animal altogether. The prospect of throwing myself into the company of a throng of strangers, and many of them probably very good golfers, was intimidating to say the least. Under most circumstances, I would run the other way just as fast as I could.

But this was different. I was starting from scratch in Arizona. I knew nobody and nobody knew me. If I were to have any semblance of a social life, I'd have to force the issue a bit. Sitting at home was not the answer. I needed to be a part of something. I needed the camaraderie. I wanted to belong. This men's golf league could be just what the doctor ordered.

It felt like a million eyes were watching me as I stood there staring down the shaft of my club at my ball sitting on the tee. I glanced one more time down the fairway. Then, with knees flexed and eyes riveted on my target, I slowly swung the club back, pausing for a split second before hurtling the black, shiny head of my driver down on the ball and connecting with a great "whoosh."

I hit it good. Oh, I felt like I had hit it good. As my body twisted gracefully, my hands swung the club around in my follow-through and I caught sight of the ball rising majestically into the air.

My heart jumped as the ball sped upward in a graceful arc. It looked good. Shouts of "good shot" and "what a hit" echoed in my ears from behind me. In that split second, standing there in my follow-through stance, I thought I had pulled it off. I had made a heck of a good shot in front of all these strangers. With my eyes riveted on my rising golf ball, I smiled.

But then, just before it reached the apex of its ascent, I watched in horror as my golf ball started to peel off to the right as if some invisible force were pulling it away from the fairway. Like a fighter jet detaching itself from the formation and flying off on its own, my ball veered way off to the right and eventually bounded off into the brush of the desert and disappeared from view.

The cheers ended abruptly. All four of us on top of the tee box stood there silently, our eyes looking into the brush in the last-known direction of the ball. Seconds passed. A gravelly voice behind me finally broke the silence. "You're gonna need a machete to find that son-of-a-bitch."

On that beautiful sunny morning, roars of laughter rose from tee box number one. After retrieving my tee from the ground, I stood up and turned around in time to see my three golfing companions hurrying down the little hill to where the carts were parked. They were smiling and laughing. "Don't worry about it," the gravelly voice continued.

This time, I could see who was speaking. He had earlier been introduced to me as Don. A short, stocky gentlemen with a huge belly hanging down over his belt, he wore a white sweater that seemed several sizes too small. I remembered watching his shot travel a good distance down the middle of the fairway only a few seconds earlier.

He smiled at me as he put his driver back in his bag. "We'll all be in there plenty of times before we're through," he said, laughing as he climbed into his cart.

I walked back to my cart a bit dejected and slid my club back into the bag. "Now don't you worry about a thing. I've, uh, I got a good bead on your ball when it landed. We'll be able to drive right to it."

Those "encouraging" words came from my golfing partner for the day, a man named Joe, who was seated in the driver's seat of the cart waiting for me to get in. "Hop in. We'll head on over there. I know right where it landed."

I plopped down on the cold plastic seat. Joe floored

the gas pedal and the cart roared off in a rush, pressing me backwards. The cool morning air blew against my face as we glided smoothly over the green grass in the direction of my ball.

"I have a knack for finding balls in the desert," said Joe as he steered the golf cart with both hands firmly on the wheel. He was a large, gregarious man, filling the space next to me with his bulk. His eyes became wide as saucers when he talked and his face was round and red. There was a very distinct Texas drawl to his speech, which proved to be somewhat unnerving to me since he would spend all day insisting that he was from Vancouver, Washington.

The cart continued on. "I've been golfing here at this golf course for a long time now and, uh…I've gotten pretty good at finding the balls," he said reassuringly. Something in my body language must have relayed a message to him.

"Don't worry," he said, taking one hand off the steering wheel and patting me sympathetically on the shoulder. "We'll find it."

I smiled at him meekly. At that moment, I wasn't worried about finding the ball. My mind was fixated on trying to figure out what I had done wrong yet again. Why did my golf balls have such an impenetrable hatred for the safety of a fairway? If this was the way it was going to go, it was going to be a long day.

We cut across the fairway and soon the cart was driving over bare dirt. Joe slowed down as he carefully maneuvered the cart around bushes, cactus, and brush. "It has to be right around this area here," Joe said as he brought the cart to a halt, dust billowing up behind us. We both got out and started poking around in the vegetation, bending low to look under the brush. We must have searched for two or three minutes, going from bush to bush, looking under and around anything that grew.

Exasperated, Joe finally wiped his brow with a forearm. "Aw, heck," he drawled. "We ain't gonna find it in here. Let's go on back to the edge of the fairway and you can drop one from there."

As the cart bumped and jolted its way back to the green grass, a sinking feeling came over me. Was this how I was going to spend my day, having my body beaten and bruised by riding over rough and tumble terrain, beating back brush with my golf club as if we were off on a wild boar hunt? Why, back home, whenever my golf ball drifted out of the fairway, all I had to do was drive over to the next fairway and calmly hit it again. But this golfing in Arizona was another world altogether.

"Here we are," Joe said, as he brought the cart to a stop on the edge of the grass. "I, uh…I would drop one right here and try again."

I got out of the cart and walked back to my bag. Reaching down into a pocket, I grabbed another ball and tossed it onto the grass a few feet away from the cart.

"Okay, so it's been awhile since I golfed," I said, pulling a three iron out and walking over to the ball. "I guess I'm a little rusty. Let's hope this shot is a better one."

Joe stood a few feet behind me with his arms folded. "Don't you worry about that," he said softly, his Texas/Vancouver drawl rising up into the morning air. "We're just out here to have fun."

Again, I stepped forward and nestled the head of the club next to the ball. After giving the fairway a long look, I reared back and swung my club, hitting the ball and sending it soaring into the sky. Up, up it went, arcing toward the center of the fairway, then at the last second, peeling away again, off to the right and landing among the brush in the desert.

"I got it! I got it!" Joe bellowed. I know right where it

went. He stood there silently, looking off into the brush for a long time. Then he turned his head and looked at me, his eyes wide with enthusiasm. "Let's head on over to my ball first so I can hit and then we'll go hunt yours down."

I climbed back into the cart, my golfing ineptitude weighing heavy on my mind. Soon we were racing off across the green grass again with the cool air in our faces. I looked over to the other side of the fairway and in the distance I could see the other two men in our foursome. They, too, were in the desert. Their cart was parked next to a large bush, and they were using their golf clubs to poke and prod around the brush. This sight should have given me some solace, letting me know that I wasn't the only one who was blundering into the desert. But I was not comforted. This place is a nightmare, I thought.

"You know, Len," Joe suddenly piped up as we careened across the fairway towards his ball. "These guys have been golfing here at this course for a long time." He was looking straight ahead with both hands on the steering wheel. "And one thing I learned from day one." We began to slow down as the cart got closer to his ball. "To golf on this course, you've got to have a lot of balls."

My eyes wandered out into the brush in the direction of where my ball had landed, in the direction of where we would soon be directing another frantic search. I opened my mouth and spoke as if I were in a trance. "In more ways than one, Joe," I said absently. "In more ways than one."

Chapter 8

THE FLEA MARKET
AND THE CHILI DOG

From the looks of things, it was going to be a long time before I would get anything to eat.

My stomach let out a low, mournful growl as my eyes scanned the items on the menu. The long line of expectant diners I'd just became a part of snaked around a set of railings, past a display of advertising posters, and finally ended in front of a window where a harried woman was frantically jotting down orders on a small, white pad. I let out a sigh and looked down at the gray cement at my feet. Yes, it was going to be a long time before I would be sitting in front of a plate of food. But then, I should have expected as much. Saturday afternoons at the Flea Market were always a circus.

The bowl of Wheaties I had heartily consumed earlier that morning had long since disappeared. My feet ached. My back was beginning to tighten up. And I was hungry. When I looked at the line of people snaking away from me, my stomach again erupted with another slow, despondent rumble.

"Have you ever had one of their chili cheese dogs?"

The friendly female voice floated through the air quite unexpectedly, cutting through my self-imposed gloom. It broke through the clamor of jumbled voices and reached my ears from somewhere behind my right shoulder.

I suddenly began to perk up. Chili cheese dog? The very words started in motion a kaleidoscope of sensory perceptions.

A juicy frank, nestled into a soft hot dog bun and smothered with gooey cheese, fresh pieces of chopped onion, and hot steaming chili floated before my eyes like a misty vision. My mouth began to water. As if in a trance, I was all but ready to reach out and grab the thing, when the soft voice broke in again.

"It sounds good. That's what I'm thinking of getting. Have you ever had one here before?"

I turned to my right. With the bustling crowd in motion behind her as a backdrop, I found myself looking into the gentle, round face of a woman who must have been all of eighty years old. She had short, curly, gray hair and wore a pair of peculiar looking glasses. The frames were dark and pointed on the sides, a style I remembered as being popular for women in the fifties and sixties. As I stood there, her eyes looked at mine expectantly.

"Ahem." I cleared my throat and blinked my eyes. "Well, no, I can't say that I have," I said, speaking loudly enough so that I could be heard over the half-dozen conversations that were in full throttle all around us. "But it does sound good, doesn't it?"

"Yes, it does," she said slowly, almost as if her utterance was an afterthought. As she spoke, her eyes left mine and she turned her attention once again to the menu printed in bold blue lettering on the wall above us. Her gaze darted from one item to the other as she bit her lower lip in concentration.

Finally, she nodded her head as if to bolster her final decision. "Well, that's what I'm going to order, a chili cheese dog." Quickly she turned around to her right and poked a little old man who was standing next to her in the ribs with her elbow. "What are you going to have, Walt?"

The poke in the ribs sent the small man staggering backwards for a step or two. He was wire thin, a couple of inches shorter than she was and, despite the warmth of the early afternoon, he was wearing, to my amazement, a long-sleeved flannel shirt buttoned up to his neck. He wore a green, well-worn baseball cap with the words "John Deere" printed on the front. Without taking his eyes off the menu above him, he grimaced slightly and rubbed his side with his left hand. "Oh, I don't know." His voice sounded tired and craggy. "We're not in any hurry, are we?"

Indeed, we were not.

I again looked down the long line of people. "No, I don't think we're in too much of a hurry here," I said to the couple. They both looked back at me with blank faces.

As I stood there, my mind wandered back to the beginning of the day. The succession of events that had brought me to this time and place had started out innocently enough with the sounds of another beautiful morning in Arizona.

I'd awakened with the day holding so much promise. Upon opening my eyes, I saw bright sunshine pouring through the windows and filling our bedroom with a river of sunlight. The birds were chirping their songs in the rose bushes just outside our window and the hum of a distant weed eater, purring its workaday sound, signaled the start of another day.

Lying there on the bed, I rubbed my eyes, stretched, and yawned. It was going to be another beautiful day, a day to relax and enjoy.

And then…

"How about we go out to the Flea Market today? There are some things I'd like to look for out there."

Uh oh, I thought. Wincing, I squeezed my eyes shut and rubbed my temples.

The happy, singsong voice was that of Diana. She was speaking loudly, trying to be heard over the water she was running in the bathroom sink.

"We could go out there and browse around a little and then have lunch. What do you think?" The sound of running water abruptly stopped and her smiling face appeared around the corner, her red hair ablaze in the sunlit room.

I looked at her without lifting my head from the pillow. Please don't do this, I thought. In my mind, I could envision the crowds and the jostling. I could picture the long lines, the traffic, and the cramped space.

Conjuring up in my mind all we would encounter at the Flea Market, I looked across the room at Diana. She was still smiling at me. Her eyes were wide with anticipation as she waited for my reply. My mind wandered for an instant. I could think of a thousand other things I would rather do that day than wade into the maelstrom that was the Flea Market.

"Sure," I said, propping myself up on my right elbow while forcing as wide a smile as I could. "That sounds like a good idea."

I was no dummy. I'd been married long enough to know I had no other option than to acquiesce.

Without a word she nodded; almost giggled, then disappeared back into the bathroom. The sound of running water resumed.

I laid back down and took a deep breath. So much for a relaxing day, I thought.

We had been there many times before, of course, the big Flea Market just off the freeway. With hundreds of vendors, it was on the must-see list of every winter visitor who would happen to set foot in the East Valley.

It was so popular, in fact, that at peak times of the snow-bird season, the Flea Market became a tangled mass of humanity which slowly flowed up and down the long aisles like some living, breathing Arizona glacier. It wound its way past tables strewn with T-shirts, baseball caps, and socks. I had often thought that the Flea Market would be a fitting place for a snowbird to meet his or her end. While searching out bargains, you could be knocked over and crushed by the stampede of frenzied shoppers, kicked aside and left to die, alone, underneath a table covered with belt buckles.

Over the years, these visits out to the Flea Market had slowly evolved, for me, into an exhausting exercise that had no real end in sight. Not unlike a dog running round and round in circles, chasing its tail in an endless display of meaningless pursuit.

On the other hand, Diana loved it. Slowly walking up and down the crowded aisles and gazing at the merchandise that, for all intents and purposes bored me to tears, for some reason made her heart soar. And no matter how uninviting these innocent little trips might have been for me, I couldn't deprive her of them.

Indeed, I dared not.

A couple of hours later, we were headed down the free-way with our car pointed east and the imposing Superstition Mountains looming up ahead. Diana, as always, had assumed her position in the passenger's seat next to me, quiet and fully engaged in her eternal paperback book. I kept my eyes on the six-lane highway ahead, making a mental note to myself that the traffic was unusually light. Cautiously, I allowed myself a fleeting, glorious thought. Perhaps the crowds at the Flea Market wouldn't be so bad today. As the car moved along the road, my mood slowly began to brighten.

My hopes were soon dashed however, when I saw the

giant traffic jam just off the freeway as we approached the exit that led to the Flea Market. Trying to suppress a frown, I flipped on the turn signal and steered our car onto the exit. Instantly, we became engulfed in a morass of bumper-to-bumper traffic, all of us inching our way along a two-lane frontage road that led to the entrance of the Flea Market.

I looked across a field at the neat rows of long, narrow, makeshift buildings. Already a sea of vehicles enveloped them, covering the parking lot with shiny cars and sun-glinted windshields. It looked like another capacity crowd.

We sat in the gridlock of the traffic jam waiting "patiently" for the chance to browse through wind chimes, flags, and flaxseed oil. I cringed inwardly as the parade inched forward. Diana calmly continued reading her book.

Finally, our car crawled into the parking lot and, after much searching, I found a parking space. Here goes, I thought, another test of human endurance. I imagined walking back to this spot a few hours later with my poor feet screaming at me, indignant that I had just made them march up and down miles of solid concrete.

Diana and I got out of the car and walked to the first building. Upon entering, we were immediately absorbed into the heaving throng of shoppers. It was like jumping into the middle of a mosh pit, voices coming from everywhere, bodies large and small bouncing off of us, whiffs of perfume and aftershave stinging my nostrils, and glimpses of mundane merchandise floating past endlessly as far as the eye could see. We instantly became one with a surging mass, all looking for the deal of the century.

In a matter of seconds, Diana was locked into shopping mode as she slowly wandered through the crowd. Her attention shifted from one side of the aisle to the other as her trained eye, disciplined from years of experience, looked for anything that might be even remotely construed as a bargain.

I knew my role in this drill perfectly by now. Stay out of sight, but not too far, and don't interfere with this process. Go slow. Browse if I must, but remain vigilant at all times. Do not lose sight of Diana and allow her to be gobbled up by the slow-moving crowd. Otherwise, the backup plan would have to be implemented which meant using our cell phones to find each other. This had happened many times in the past, and I tried to avoid it because it only added to the confusion.

And so it went, minute after minute, yard after excruciating yard. We marched with measured steps up and down the aisles, Diana occasionally stopping to look at something, then waving for me to come over. After weaving through the human obstacle course to get to her side, I would nod and say all the right words. Yes, it looks pretty. Yes, that is nice. Yes, it would look good in our kitchen, bathroom, or bedroom, whatever the case may be. Invariably, these exchanges would end with Diana scrunching up her nose, slowly shaking her head, and then putting the thing back down on the table, as if any input I might have made had been meaningless, which in truth, it was.

As time would wear on though, bags would eventually be thrust in my direction. One, then two, then more. Our slow march up and down the aisles of merchandise would soon be accompanied by several plastic bags filled with "stuff" bumping against the sides of my legs with my fingers entwined around their plastic handles. Sometimes, I would walk by other men in the same situation, their hands similarly full of bags. Our eyes would meet for a few seconds and we would give each other a subtle nod, acknowledging the bond that held us together as a band of brothers.

At the Flea Market, I considered myself a gamer. I would hang in there as long as I could. But eventually, I would need to get off my feet for a while. "I'm going up ahead and find a place to sit down," I would tell Diana. Fully engrossed in some sort of article she had in her hand, she would nod silently without looking at me, and I would be off on my mission, bags dangling by my side.

The rarest of rare commodities at the Flea Market was the tantalizing sight of an empty space on a bench. I suppose one could argue that it was harder to find than the Lost Dutchman's Mine for which the Superstition Mountains are so famous. For some reason, my fellow brethren always seemed to be one step ahead of me in filling up every inch of these priceless sections real estate. Before I could find someplace to sit down, I would have to pass by bench after bench filled with men, their full plastic bags sitting on the ground by their sides.

I became adept at reading their faces. Those who looked utterly exhausted I would pass by rapidly knowing that it would be a long time before they would be on their feet again. Why waste my time? I was looking for the face with the well rested look. And when I did find one, I would inconspicuously loiter nearby, ready to pounce into their spot at a moment's notice. Once seated, I would put my bags down in front of me, lean back and fold my arms, comforted in the fact that it would be a long time before I would see Diana idly walking by, which would signal my return once again to the march.

On this day, however, the appearance of Diana happily strolling by my bench was met with a low growl deep within my abdomen and a sudden realization that all this walking around had worked up an enormous appetite.

"Hey, you," I half-shouted as Diana got within earshot of me from my perch on the bench.

She turned. Her face lit up when she saw me. Obviously, she was having a good time. "There you are. I've been looking all over for you."

"What do you think about going to get something to eat? I'm getting hungry."

"You know, I was just thinking the same thing," she said, brushing her hair with her hand. "I'm starting to get hungry myself."

We made our way through the crowd to the lunch area. When we arrived, we stopped and looked out in dismay as our eyes swept across the thirty or so full tables in front of us and a forest of people standing around waiting to sit down. To our left, there was a long line waiting to order at the window. Loud conversation was everywhere.

"Why don't I go order for us both?" I asked gallantly. "You wait here and grab a table when someone leaves." I had to raise my voice over some loud music that was coming from a young keyboard player over in the corner.

She nodded as I handed her the bags. "Get me whatever you're having," she said. I turned and walked over to the end of the line.

The old lady with the pointed glasses spoke again as I gazed up above me at the menu. "Where are you from?" she asked.

"Idaho."

"Idaho, huh?" The woman gave the wiry old man next to her another jolt in the ribs with her elbow. "Hey, Walt! These folks are from Idaho. What do you think about that?"

Trying valiantly to regain his balance from the second jolt, he grimaced and grabbed his side. "Idaho? I think we passed through there once or twice," he wheezed. Rubbing his side with his left hand, his eyes widened as he let out a long, slow breath.

The woman turned back to me and I could see in her

face that a thought had just crossed her mind. "Say, I don't suppose you're going tell us that you grow potatoes." She started chuckling at her little joke and looked over at Walt.

For a second, his face conveyed an expression of panic and he quickly stepped back a step or two. When he saw he wasn't going to get it in the ribs again, he started chuckling with her as well. "Yeah, that would be funny, growing potatoes in Idaho."

I stared at them without expression. They both looked at me as they smiled and chuckled. When they saw I wasn't joining in on their merriment, their quiet laughter slowly subsided until they were standing there wordlessly clearing their throats.

Giving them my best smile, I said. "You're not going to believe this, but as a matter of fact, I am a potato farmer. That's what I do for a living."

"Well, I'll be," the woman said slowly, her mouth dropping open. She turned to her husband.

Again he took an involuntary step backwards with a wary eye on the woman, his hands held up in front of him for protection. "That's really something," he said. "Who would've ever thought?"

"Okay, now it's your turn," I said. "Where are you folks from?"

"Who, us?" The woman's eyes widened as if she had never been asked that question before. "Oh, we're from North Dakota."

My eyebrows arched upwards. North Dakota! I was just about to tell them that my wife had been born in North Dakota, when my cell phone began ringing a rollicking Jamaican melody.

"Excuse me," I said, hurriedly reaching into my pants pocket to pull out the cell phone. "Hello?"

Diana's irritated voice crackled in my ear. "What's taking you so long?"

"Well, I, uh, I'm just standing here in line, waiting like everyone else."

"Well, I don't know how much longer I can hold this table."

"What do you mean?"

"People are really starting to give me the evil eye, you know, me sitting here all alone without any food in front of me."

"I see. Yes, that could be a problem." My mind conjured up an unruly mob with pitchforks and torches circling the table and staring down at Diana, while she courageously sat there steadfast. I imagined her looking up at them with fear in her eyes.

"Well, do the best you can," I said, trying to sound as encouraging as possible. "It won't be too much longer."

"Well, just hurry up." With that, the cell phone went silent.

Putting the phone back in my pocket, I looked up and saw that there were only two people between me and the window now. It wouldn't be long. I hoped Diana could hold out just a few minutes more.

Turning to the couple behind me, I resumed our conversation. "My wife was born in North Dakota."

This seemed to really liven up the old couple. They asked me where, and I told them. They said that they only live an hour or so away from there. Then the man, who had been rather quiet and shy, possibly fearful of more jolts to the ribs, truly opened up and spent the next few minutes telling me of his farm, how he had retired from there eleven years ago, and that his son was now running the place. He reminisced about the crops he had grown and the cattle he had raised, all the while smiling wistfully and occasionally reaching a bony hand underneath his "John Deere" cap to scratch his head.

The conversation made time move fast. Soon we all had our food and were carrying trays filled with chili cheese dogs towards the condiment bar. "It was so nice talking to you," the lady said, looking at me through her pointed glasses. "Maybe we'll meet again somewhere down the road."

"I hope so," I said. "It was very nice chatting with you, too."

After getting some ketchup and mustard and onions and relish, I entered the crowded seating area and saw Diana sitting at a table in the back, waving at me. I zigzagged my way toward her through the crowd.

"I'm never going to do this again," she said as I reached the table and set the tray down in front of her. "Next time, I'm going to get in line with you."

"Yeah, that probably wasn't a good idea." I looked at the knots of people standing around us like vultures waiting for tables to become available. I silently hoped it would be a long time before the next time. "We'll do that differently when we come here again," I promised.

I sat down and eyed the steaming chili cheese dog in front of me, rubbing my palms together. I put a good-sized chunk into my mouth with a plastic fork. Mmmmmm, heavenly. Closing my eyes, I savored the taste. This had made the long wait worth it.

Diana and I ate like ravenous wolves, completely lost in the moment. But it wasn't long before I noticed, between bites, that a couple of people were standing uncomfortably close to us, watching and waiting. I tried not to look at them, but the message was clear. Someone wanted us to hurry up.

Just when my chili cheese dog was half gone and I was

chomping down on another glorious bite, I felt a finger gently tapping me on my shoulder from behind.

"Excuse me, you don't mind if we join you while you eat, do you? We're waiting for our husbands to order and you'll be done long before they get here."

I turned to see two women, early sixties, each wearing pants and sweaters looking down at us in a pleading fashion.

Diana and I stopped chewing and stared up at them, surprised more than anything else at their entreaty, an awkward moment to say the least.

Finally, Diana, one who always made friends with anyone anywhere, broke the silence. "Sure, sure, we'd be happy to have you join us. Sit down. Sit down. There's plenty of room for two more."

Almost giddy with delight, the two women sat down beside us while we scooted sideways to the edge of our bench and pulled our chili cheese dogs along with us.

"Oh, thank you. Thank you so much," the first woman said. "We have been so worried about finding a place to sit since our husbands got in line. I was afraid we were going to have to find some place to eat standing up."

"Oh, yes," the second woman chimed in. "That would've been so uncomfortable. We're so grateful for letting us sit here with you."

I took another bite of my chili cheese dog while the two newcomers continued to hold court.

"This place is so crowded," the first woman continued. "I just don't know what we were going to do if you hadn't let us sit here."

Diana and I, with our mouths too full to engage in any conversation right at that moment, just sat in silence and finished eating while the two women talked. And talked.

"We just got here the other day from Iowa," the second

woman continued. "I'm so glad to get out of that horrible winter weather for a few weeks. But we can't stay long. Oh, no. Our husbands have to get back to work. Insurance business, you know."

"I see," I managed to say through a mouthful of chili cheese dog.

"By the way, where are you folks from?"

Diana swallowed and then took a long drink of soda. "Idaho," she finally managed to say as she wiped her mouth with a napkin.

"Oh!"

"Say isn't that where they grow all those potatoes?" the first woman piped up.

With a teasing look in her eye, the second woman turned to me and grinned. "I don't suppose you're going to tell us that you're a potato farmer, now are you?"

At that, both women looked at each other and broke out laughing in high-pitched giggles.

Here we go again, I thought. It had been a long day. My feet hurt. My back ached. Ahead of me lay a long hike back to the car with a load of bags to carry. And now I was being interrogated by a couple of women from Iowa while I tried to eat. I privately vowed that it would be a long time before I came back here again.

I closed my eyes and continued chewing, trying to savor every last morsel. Reluctantly, I finally swallowed the final bite of a meal for which I had just waited twenty minutes in line.

I looked over at the two women and waited for their laughter to die down, my standard response to their question waiting wearily on the tip of my tongue.

Chapter 9

DOWN MEXICO WAY

The room was large and spacious, easily accommodating our busload of snowbirds. Elegant oriental symbols and décor adorned the dining hall as we sat at two long tables chatting and waiting to be served. Our tour guide had promised us that our last lunch in Mexico would be a unique experience. She'd said we would be dining at an exclusive Chinese restaurant that had very good food and lots of it.

This was good enough for me. I took her at her word. My Mexican breakfast of eggs and refried beans back at the hotel had long since disappeared, and I was ready to eat.

It had felt good to get off the bus and stretch my legs after the two-hour trip from San Felipe to Mexicali. This was the last leg of our bus tour, a three-day trip down the Baja Peninsula along the Sea of Cortez. While it had been fun to travel and see new things, I was looking forward to sleeping in my own bed that night.

At my table were my three traveling companions of the last three days: Diana, her brother Larry, and his wife Glenda. We had been like a close-knit group of schoolmates out on a field trip. We had shared practically every meal, wandered together in the same shops, and scavenged collectively on the beach for sand dollars. But this would be our last meal together in this role and the feeling of conclusion hung over us.

Then I saw them. They appeared out of nowhere from the far side of the room. Oh no, I thought. Not again. Like a well-trained troupe, a platoon of waiters entered the room each carrying a large tray covered with tall, long-stemmed glasses filled with the signature drink of Mexico. It was the obligatory free, first margarita.

One of the waiters, a short, round, dark-haired man, was heading in our direction. He walked with purpose, holding the tray in front of him and weaving around the other tables with a style that belied his appearance. When he reached our table, he sat our margaritas down with a flair that seemed to imply he'd been anxiously awaiting all day for this very moment.

My eyes followed his hand from tray to table as he placed the tall goblet-like glass in front of me. The green, icy liquid sloshed ever so slightly as the glass made contact with the white tablecloth. Like a proud sentinel, the margarita stood there, taunting me. The thick ring of salt around the rim glistened under the lights of the room. Others reached for their drinks and began sipping, but I held back, eyeing my drink with an admiration and respect given only to the most worthy of opponents. As if tired by the wait, the margarita let loose a small droplet of water, which began slowly running down the side of the glass.

So…I thought, looking at the margarita. We meet again I see. Well, not so fast my cocky little friend. This time it's going to be different. This time I'm ready for your wily subtle charms, your icy green stare, and your salty rimmed seductive dance. I reached for the glass of ice water sitting next to the margarita and took a long sip, as if to prove that I had broken free and found someone new. Eyeing the margarita again, I smiled reassuringly, returning the glass of water to the table. This time you will not lure me into your trap.

I had been emotionally ready for this moment since the disaster of two days ago in San Felipe. I had been blindsided then, not realizing that a margarita in Mexico was not, and I repeat, not the same innocuous drink that I had been occasionally ordering with dinner for the last thirty-some years back home in the States. Oh no. Not the same at all.

The idea for this trip to Mexico had begun one night a couple of months earlier with a phone call. It was Glenda calling from their winter home in Yuma, wondering if we would like to go with them on a bus trip into Mexico. We had been on several joint ventures with them already during the past snowbird season and another excursion into the unknown sounded like fun.

Thus began a waiting period that encompassed many more phone calls between Diana and Glenda as they planned, talked, and fussed about the impending trip. Although I didn't ask, I was able to detect from Diana's side of the conversation that the overriding issues were what to wear, what to do, what to see. As the big day closed in on us, the level of phone chatter between the two increased.

Finally, the big day arrived. After an overnight stay at their place in Yuma, the four of us found ourselves climbing aboard a big tour bus at eight o'clock on a cool, cloudy morning. Glenda, always the adventuresome one, was a bundle of energy as we settled in for the ride. "This is gonna be so neat, you guys," she said as she looked at me and Diana from across the aisle, her smile filling the bus. "A few days on the beach, eating out every meal, looking for sand dollars, it's gonna be awesome."

"I hope it doesn't rain on us," Larry said, peering up into the sky through the side window.

"What the heck?" Diana chimed in. "Even if it rains a little bit, we're still gonna have a good time seeing something we've never seen before."

Soon we were on our way. We were sitting in the third seat from the front. The inside of the bus was busy with conversation as we rolled away from the parking lot and out onto the freeway, heading to the Mexican border. I looked behind me and saw that the bus was completely full, a snowbird in every seat.

Once inside Mexico, the ride to San Felipe covered vast emptiness. The desert that was soon hurtling past my window was scattered thinly with cactus and brush. It stretched on for miles. From my seat, I could see the back of the driver's balding head as he pawed the enormous steering wheel in front of him. The straight and empty two-lane road stretched endlessly out the huge front window.

Traffic was light, almost nonexistent. As I sat in my seat, feeling the bus jostle along the road, I could easily tell how much of a priority road building was to the Mexican government. This was the narrowest two-lane road I had ever seen in my life. There was no shoulder and it appeared that there had been no grading done along the side of the road at all. To make matters worse, the large bus barely fit in the right lane. I could turn my head and look down the side of the bus and see that there was nowhere to go if, God forbid, we had to swerve off the road for some reason. Nowhere to go, that is, but drop off into the bleak Mexican desert. Sitting there with the bus rumbling beneath me, I tried to think of something else.

Our hostess, a tall blonde woman in her mid-sixties who sat only two seats in front of me, had been whetting our appetite all morning with little facts about San Felipe and what we could expect when we got there. Every time she wanted to say something, she had the annoying habit of keying the microphone and tapping on it a few times before she spoke. The loud, intermittent…THUMP…THUMP…THUMP… crackling from the speakers and echoing throughout the bus would become our cue that an important announcement was about to follow.

THUMP…THUMP…THUMP

"Folks, for those of you who will have a room on the second floor of the hotel, please be careful walking up the stairs. The stairs in Mexico are not like our stairs in the United States. They are uneven and they are not all the same height. So please be conscious of that and watch your step as you walk up to your room, particularly tonight in the dark. We want all of you to have a good time, but we don't want to see anyone get hurt."

The passengers rode along in silence letting this announcement sink in. How odd, I thought. How hard is it to build a staircase that's even? Don't they have measuring tapes in Mexico? While I tried to digest this bit of information, I noticed that we were entering into a slightly mountainous area. The approaching hills were bare of any trees and they rose up abruptly from the desert floor. Beyond the hills, I could see for the first time off to our left, a body of water, presumably the Sea of Cortez. We must be getting close, I thought.

THUMP…THUMP…THUMP

"Folks, I just want you to know that if you walk into town to do some shopping or to check out the restaurants, please be aware that the curbs in Mexico are not like the curbs we have in the United States. They are very uneven and sometimes rather high, much higher than we are accustomed to back home. So please watch your step so you don't fall and hurt yourself while walking downtown."

What the heck is going on here, I thought, as the bus continued on across the isolated stretch of road. I conjured up in my mind, broken bodies of tourists lying scattered all over San Felipe, crying out for emergency medical attention because their tour guide didn't have the foresight to warn them in advance of the hazards that would befall them in this apparently inhospitable town. I looked at our hostess sitting ramrod straight in her seat, looking at her clipboard, evidently searching for the next warning to give her charges. Either she was the most paranoid person I had ever seen or she was saving all of our lives. At the moment, I didn't know which.

Soon the Sea of Cortez, named after the Spanish conquistador who conquered the region in the 1500s, became more visible on our left. Buildings began to crop up intermittently on either side of the road and traffic began to pick up. Then the bus turned a rare corner and, going around a rise, I could see a short distance away a couple of official looking vehicles off to the side of the road. A small group of men, four or five perhaps, was standing next to the vehicles. They were dressed in military clothing, shouldering rifles, and smoking cigarettes. The bus driver slowly applied the brakes and the bus began rolling to a stop.

THUMP...THUMP...THUMP

"Ladies and gentlemen, we will have to stop at this checkpoint. Please listen carefully. For the next few minutes, it is time to be very serious. When the gentleman comes on the bus, look straight ahead and don't say anything. Don't laugh. Don't talk. Don't joke around and say something stupid like 'We're on a drug run' or something like that, or these men will empty this bus and we'll be standing alongside the road for the next six hours while they tear the bus apart. So please, just sit still and be quiet for a few minutes, and then we'll be on our way."

The bus rolled to a stop and our tour guide stood up and took a step over to the driver's seat and stood next to the driver. The door opened and a man wearing green military fatigues with a rifle slung over his shoulder came on the bus. He stopped and said something in Spanish to both the driver and the tour guide and they nodded. He turned his head and looked at us anxiously. Again, he said something in Spanish and looked at the driver and our hostess. They again both silently nodded in unison. I couldn't help but be amazed at the youth of this man. Actually, he wasn't a man at all, but rather a boy. He seemed no older than sixteen or seventeen.

From my seat, I could see the rest of the men in the group standing outside. They were all young, although not quite as young as the man on our bus. They didn't seem to be concerned at all with what was going on inside of our bus. They were smiling and joking around with each other.

The man on our bus stood in the front and just looked at us for the longest time as if he were trying to recognize a familiar face. Again, I was struck by his youth. It was unthinkable to imagine a boy of this age back home in the States to be legally imposing his will on a busload of adults with a rifle slung over his shoulder. We all sat still as statues, looking straight ahead, not knowing what was going to happen next.

Without saying a word, the young man started walking slowly down the aisle looking from one side to the other. He walked right by me. I could smell the cigarette smoke on his clothes. His rifle brushed my shoulder as he went past. His black, high-top boots made an ominous sound as he made his way slowly and deliberately to the back of the bus. All the passengers seemed to be holding their breath.

Then the footsteps quickened. He was headed towards the front again, this time much faster. It was as if he'd decided that whatever he was looking for was not on the bus. He walked past me briskly and for the first time since he boarded, he smiled. "Gracias," he said as he nodded in the direction of the driver and our tour guide.

"Gracias," they answered together as the man quickly exited the bus.

Our tour guide took her seat and the bus driver closed the door. The bus started rolling again and we all looked at each other, not knowing what to think.

Diana turned to me. "What do you suppose that was all about?" she asked, in a low, hushed voice.

"Who knows?" I replied. "Probably something to do with drugs."

I believe we were all a little shaken by the incident, but our hostess and the bus driver appeared unfazed by it all. I got the impression that this was a frequent and boring experience for them. All in a day's work. No announcement was made. No explanation was given. Soon the bus had reached cruising speed again, and it was as if it had never happened.

In a few minutes we started down a short incline and I could see below us the town of San Felipe framed against the blue waters of the Sea of Cortez. The sight was like an oasis after the long, monotonous ride. Like thirsty cattle finally arriving at the watering hole, the passengers came alive with interest and strained to get a better look.

We entered town through an attractive double arch, apparently put there for public relations purposes. The two arches stood together spanning each lane on the highway. One arch was slightly taller than the other, giving the design an abstract feel. I looked past the driver's head through the large front window as the archway loomed in front of us and then it disappeared behind us as we passed through it. This was the symbol of San Felipe, the one tourists saw on the posters and brochures.

As the bus made its way through the streets, I noticed

that the buildings were old and in disrepair. It appeared that at least every other structure that went past my window was neglected or abandoned or both. Discarded tires and piles of old bricks were strewn about haphazardly throughout the town, and there was a general dinginess about the place. Each house had a lot of clutter around it. The prevailing atmosphere was one of dreariness. It began to dawn on me that the most modern looking structure I'd seen so far had been the arch.

From high up in the bus I could see that there were a few cars on the streets, and most of those were older models and they were usually belching smoke behind them. The town was empty of pedestrians with no sign of anyone out and about on foot. The only living things that were walking along the streets were dogs. Most were tall and skinny, just wandering around on their own without any sign of a master in tow.

The bus made a right turn just a block or two before the seashore. The engine roared as the driver shifted gears and we made our way past a row of hotels. This street was in sharp contrast to the part of town that we had just passed through with about four or five nice looking hotel buildings lined up along the beach. We pulled into the parking lot of the last hotel on the street. It was a Spanish style building with a lot of arches and an attractive red-tiled roof. Our bus slowly rolled to a stop in front of the curb.

THUMP...THUMP...THUMP

"Ladies and gentlemen, welcome to San Felipe and the hotel El Cortez. After you have checked into your room, the management of the hotel invites you to the Barefoot Bar for a free margarita. The bar is the building on the beach just across from the hotel. The bartender is expecting you. Just tell him you are from the bus tour. Everyone, please enjoy yourselves and once again, welcome to San Felipe."

This was the first time that an announcement didn't also include some word of caution about tripping over something and hurting ourselves. I was relieved.

Diana and I got up out of our seats and made our way to the door. The breeze was cool against my face as I stepped off the bus and onto the blacktop. I could smell the sea in the air. Our driver, a quiet fellow wearing a gray company jacket that said "Harris Tours" on the front, had already retrieved everyone's belongings from underneath the bus and was dutifully standing next to the assortment of luggage on the ground. As the rest of the crowd milled about looking for their bags, we retrieved our suitcases and checked into our room.

Chapter 10

SOUSED OF THE BORDER

After freshening up a bit in our room, Diana and I walked alone across the quiet plaza to the small red building. The Barefoot Bar was only fifty yards or so from the hotel and located right on the beach. I thought it was too early yet to expect a lot of people from our bus to be there, and we were looking forward to a quiet drink before the crowd arrived.

When we reached the entrance, I pulled open the tall wooden door and we were met with a blast of deafening music. The place was packed. I could see that most of the people there were fellow passengers from our bus. Tables were surrounded by happy faces and everyone was laughing and drinking. We stood there at the door looking around the crowded room. How did all these people get here so fast? Apparently, the free margarita couldn't wait. It took a while for our eyes to adjust to the bar's dim interior. In the back of the room, I could see two arms waving back and forth. Larry and Glenda had wasted no time in getting to the party.

We started making our way through the crowded bar, meandering around tables and trying to avoid colliding with waitresses carrying trays laden with margaritas. As we got closer to the back of the room, Larry spotted us struggling towards them. "What took you so long?" he shouted over the music.

"Are you kidding?" I shouted back above the din. "We were only in our room for a few minutes. You must have run over here." As I said this, I noticed for the first time the source of the booming disco music. It was a big screen TV in the corner, showing girls in bikinis dancing on a beach.

Larry chuckled as he took a sip of his margarita. "Heck, all we did was put our suitcases in the room and then make a beeline for this place." He smiled and took another long sip from the straw that was sticking out of the top of his drink.

Larry was an imposing figure. A bear of a man to begin with, his frame dwarfed the small bamboo weave chair in which he was sitting. The cane he always had to use to support a bad knee was leaning against his leg. With his tropical shirt pulled casually out over the top of his Bermuda shorts, he looked right at home.

"They got your free margaritas up at the bar," he said, waving his drink in the air. "You better go get one. You've got a lot of catching up to do." He laughed as he took another drink.

I could feel a warmness entering me as I looked down at Larry sitting there, happy as a clam. It was a welcome feeling I always got in his presence. Larry exuded fun. Being around him had always made me feel good. No matter what was going on in life, a few minutes with Larry and any problems you had would be put on a shelf.

The margarita tasted like honey. Our table faced a large window which was open to the beach. While Diana, Glenda, and Larry engaged in small talk, I leaned back in my chair and slowly descended into a dreamy stupor while I sipped on my straw, gazing out at the Sea of Cortez. The soft blue waters rushed out to the horizon to meet the endless sky. I was lost in its beauty. I was lost in the luscious taste of the margarita. I was lost in the moment.

We ordered another round, then another. Time suddenly meant nothing. The bar was now filled with the sound of boisterous laughter and loud conversation as the margaritas spun their magic on the crowd. The music flooded the room as the pounding disco beat dominated the atmosphere.

I looked at the large TV screen in the corner, the source of the pulsating music. The picture never seemed to change. There were always girls wearing bikinis and dancing on a beach. Sometimes different girls, sometimes a different beach, but always bikinis, dancing, and music. The voiceover was in Spanish, so I had no idea what they were talking about. Finally, after much studied concentration through hazy eyes, I was able to discern that what I was watching was a series of commercials for a Mexican beer. As I sipped my margaritas, the dancing bikini girls on the enormous screen above me soon became my primary focus.

The margaritas were in full effect now. It was hard to pull my eyes away from the TV. Time had become irrelevant. Isn't it interesting, I thought, how many different colors there were of bikinis. I stared at the TV, ruminating on this educated observation for a moment, sipping the sweet liquid through my straw. The margaritas, the music, the dancing, the jiggling were all getting to me when another observation popped into my head.

And isn't it also interesting, I thought, that there are so many different sizes of…

It was then that I heard, ever so faintly through the racket in the bar, someone calling my name. It was Larry.

I felt my lips move. I'm pretty sure they did, but I can't be certain because by this time they felt thick and somewhat numb. "I'm sorry, did you say something?" I asked.

Larry was looking at me expectantly. "I said, would you like another margarita before we head downtown and have a look around?"

I looked down at my drink. To my surprise, it was almost empty. I looked back at Larry and nodded. In an instant he was off, his large frame moving in the direction of the bar. My gaze returned to the TV. I felt as if I were in a dream.

I've never been much of a drinker. Having learned years ago that I was a cheap drunk, I usually was smart enough to stop before things got too far out of hand. But for some reason, this time was different. These margaritas had crept up on me in a matter of only a few minutes and had quickly overwhelmed my otherwise trusty defense mechanism. And besides, they tasted so darned good.

The cold, icy liquid of the new margarita glided far too easily and pleasantly down my throat. I took the tip of my index finger, wet from holding the glass, rubbed some of the salt off the rim, and put it on my tongue. I washed it down with another glorious sip. I leaned back in my chair and happily took stock of my surroundings. With the bikinis, the music, the dancing, the laughter, and the sea, this little bar on the beach had been transformed into the happiest place on earth.

A few minutes later, there was some motion from Larry's side of the table. "Well, we'd better get going, bud," he said as he slapped me on leg and rose from his chair. "Let's go see what's going on downtown."

My eyes opened wide as I grabbed the straw and slurped down the last drops of my margarita. I set the empty glass down on the table and attempted to rise up from the chair. I hadn't moved from this spot in over an hour, and now I felt as though I weighed a ton. Larry steadied his huge frame with his ever present cane as he led the way toward the door. I had to give myself a pep talk just to keep from crashing into someone's table. *Come on now, Len. You can do it. Just put one foot in front of the other. Easy, easy, you can make it. Follow Larry, head for the door.*

The four of us left the bar and walked outside into the cool air. Soon the bar's music began to fade in the distance.

We crossed over the plaza and walked through the parking lot of the hotel. The sight of our bus parked off to the side, towering over the surroundings like a great beast, was rather reassuring to my bleary eyes. Its presence there, grounded me in some strange way and gave me a feeling of comfort, knowing that no matter what was going to happen next, we could always count on the big bus to take us home, back to the States, eventually.

As Larry led the way with his plodding gait, cane in hand, we turned a corner and I could see shops and bars down the road a couple of blocks away. The streets were empty of both cars and pedestrians.

It was still the middle of the afternoon, which struck me as somewhat odd. Although it had been decades since I had last stumbled around half smashed, even then it had been in the dead of night, and always in the company of equally smashed and equally youthful friends. As I lurched along behind Larry, Glenda, and Diana, I noticed that they seemed perfectly fine, as if they hadn't had a drop to drink. What was wrong with me, I wondered. Why were they walking, talking, and acting like normal people while I could hardly stand up?

"I hope we find some bargains," said Glenda as we approached an intersection. "I love to dicker with the peddlers."

"Well you're gonna get your chance," Larry said over his shoulder. "There's a whole street full of 'em up here."

"I'd like to find a T-shirt," Diana said, "Something to take home as a souvenir."

Walking along behind them, I tried to think of something – anything – I could say to include myself in the conversation. Reaching back into my muddled mind, through the margarita-induced haze, I searched for some words, but none were forthcoming. I gave up and continued to stumble along behind them in silence.

Just as we came to an empty intersection, an incredible thing happened. It was like something out of a movie. I stood there in shock as the three figures in front of me dropped suddenly out of sight. It was as if they'd fallen through a trapdoor. Then I looked down and saw the tops of their three heads quickly moving away from me as I came to a halt, wobbling precariously at the top of an enormous curb.

This was the tallest curb I had ever seen in my life. How my three companions had nonchalantly stepped down off the sidewalk and continued on their way, I will never know. Maybe the margaritas were playing tricks on me, but I felt as if I might as well have been standing on the precipice of an abyss.

Larry, Glenda, and Diana continued on through the intersection talking and walking with no regard for my predicament. Gingerly, I lowered my left foot down into the yawning chasm, trying to find the bottom. But almost immediately, I began to lose my balance and I quickly brought my foot back up again, arms flailing. I glanced ahead of me and saw that my companions were almost on the other side of the street. I began to panic.

Again, I tentatively lowered my leg into the great gulf with the same result. I quickly lifted it back up once more, whirling my arms around as if I were a circus tightrope act. Now I'm really in a fix, I thought.

It would be embarrassing to call out to them. I shook my head as I watched the three of them continue on their merry way. No, I couldn't call for help. I mean, how would I ever live that down? Our two-day stay in San Felipe had just begun. I didn't want to be the highlight of our trip only an hour into it.

Then, like a beacon of hope shining out of the foggy depths, I had a thought. After first glancing around to see if anyone was watching, I slowly bent down. With my hands and knees on the cold cement, I lowered my left foot until it touched the solid pavement below. Then I lowered my right foot, and then awkwardly stood up.

I could only imagine what that must have looked like. Concerned about that, I turned around again to make certain no one had seen me. To my drunken delight, as far as I could see, no one had witnessed my embarrassing moment. I brushed myself off and hurried the best I could to catch up with the others.

We were soon deep in the heart of the tourist area with shops, bars, and restaurants lining both sides of the street. Larry's deliberate pace slowed considerably as everyone started browsing through the tables of curios and the tons of clothing hanging along the sidewalk.

"We really have to get something for the grandkids, Larry," Glenda said as she rummaged through some T-shirts and jackets.

"Yeah, I know," Larry mumbled as he slowly walked past the merchandise.

As we were making our way down the sidewalk, I almost bumped into Larry when he stopped suddenly after something caught his eye. He was looking at a small wooden turtle on the table in front of him. He reached down and flicked its head with his finger. The turtle's head slowly bobbed up and down. We both laughed at the funny sight. The turtle was sitting among other turtles of different sizes and colors. To our amusement, we soon had numerous turtles going bonkers with their heads as our fingers worked feverishly to keep them bobbing up and down. We both couldn't stop laughing at the sight. The margaritas, of course, no doubt helped make all of this funnier than it probably was.

Larry's smile suddenly vanished from his face as he whipped around to confront a salesman. "How much?" he asked seriously.

A young, dark man who'd been hovering by our side for the last several minutes, stepped forward. He looked at us eagerly, ready to engage yet another customer in the time-honored Mexican custom of establishing a price for the sale of goods. But Larry was ready. He gravely looked at the young man with his jaw set in a fierce look of determination. Larry had now been transformed into full-blown bargaining mode.

"Oh, these are very fine turtles, sir," the man said in broken English, talking rapidly and waving his hands about in great, sweeping gestures. "You will not find a better quality turtle in all of Mexico. I will sell these turtles for you today, only four dollar each." The young man stepped back and folded his arms, regarding us impassively. A slight smile creased his lips. It was as if he had just offered us a share in a huge and profitable Mexican conglomerate. The ball was clearly in our court.

"Four bucks, huh?" Larry leaned on his cane and rubbed his chin thoughtfully. Then he turned to the young man. "That's too much. I want Wal-Mart prices." With that, Larry threw back his head and let loose one of his wonderful belly laughs. This apparently seemed to have made his day. Then he turned and walked away, leaving the perplexed young man standing by himself with the turtles.

We left the sidewalk displays and wandered into the interior of a store where we saw the girls standing by a rack of jackets appraising the stock. "How do you like this jacket, Glenda?" Diana asked as she held up a gray hooded parka with the words "San Felipe" printed on the back alongside the design of a sailboat.

"Oh, that's pretty!" Glenda gasped as she walked closer to get a better look.

Instantly, a small, swarthy man stepped out of the shadows and approached the women. "Good afternoon, señoras. You like?" He pointed to the jacket.

I stood off to the side, holding myself up against a table. Here it comes, I thought. Glenda had been talking about this moment for weeks. She loved the wrangle and was not about to walk out of that store, any store in Mexico, with an overpriced piece of merchandise. I leaned back with my arms folded, anticipating the cat and mouse game that was to follow.

"Well, yeah, I guess." Glenda held the jacket up by the hanger at arm's length. "How much?"

"Today, special price," the man said in very broken English. "Normally, thirty-five American dollars, but for you?" He paused for a moment. "For you? Twenty-five."

Glenda looked as if she had been shot. "Oh no, no," she said emphatically as she slammed the hanger back onto the hook, the jacket shaking in the aftershock.

"But señora." The man looked as though his dog had just died. "This jacket is finest quality, made in Guadalajara, shipped special for San Felipe customers."

Glenda was unyielding. "Yeah, yeah. Whatever. I can buy the same thing in Algadones for ten." And with that she started to walk away.

"Wait, wait," the man said as we started to leave the store. "In Algadones, there are no San Felipe jackets."

Glenda stopped and thought a moment. "Well, no, I guess not," she said.

"Today, I make special price for you," the man said with

great display, holding both hands out. "You buy two jackets, one for you, one for husband. You pay only twenty each." The man leaned back on his heels and waited .

The counteroffer was swift and immediate. "Fifteen!" demanded Glenda.

The man winced and his shoulders sagged. Feigning a look of defeat, he nodded his head and began folding the jackets and putting them in a plastic sack.

"Gracias," the man said with a wry smile as he handed her the bag.

Glenda chuckled softly as she handed the man thirty dollars and grabbed the bag. As we walked out the door, I wondered, even in my smashed state, just who had gotten the better of that deal.

We left the shop and wandered out into the street. Larry spotted a bar across the way. It was a cheerful looking place with the door facing the street splashed with bright green paint and an attractive sign inviting us into "The Green Door".

"Hey, anybody game for another margarita?" Larry asked as he pointed his cane in that direction, not waiting for an answer. We crossed the street as if we were on a mission with Larry leading the way.

We entered the little bar. It was devoid of customers, and soon we were sitting at a table with the largest margaritas I had ever seen. I reached up to pull the drink closer to me and both of my hands barely fit around the cold, wet glass. Still reeling from the last round of drinks back at the Barefoot Bar, I doubted whether I could finish the mammoth margarita. And even if I did, I wondered if I would live to tell about it. Nevertheless, I slowly began sipping down the luscious liquid while we sat there and talked.

The rest of the afternoon remains a bit hazy to me even to this day. Only bits and pieces of it come back to me from time to time. Oh, I finished the huge margarita all right, sitting there chatting and watching its contents slowly get lower and lower with every sip I took.

My memory of the walk back to the hotel is also pretty sketchy. I remember making the walk, much like the way we came, Larry lumbering steadily along with his cane and the rest of us following. During most of the walk back, I was carrying a plastic bag that I later found out held a San Felipe shirt, which means I must have bought a T-shirt at some point. To this day I shudder to think of how I must have looked during that purchase.

The image does come back to me once in a while of Larry standing on the edge of a high cliff, reaching his cane down to me, and pulling me up to safety amid peals of laughter from the group. I wasn't surprised to learn that the scratches on my arms, which I nursed for days afterwards, were caused by this incident.

I do remember bursting through the door of our hotel room and belly flopping onto the bed, lying there motionless while the room spun round and round. Diana kept circling me while brushing her hair and saying, "Come on, Len. You'd better get ready for dinner. Our hostess has a reservation for our tour group at a nice steakhouse downtown."

I remember lying there on the bed with my face squished against the pillow, my eyes staring vacantly at the window shades. "Do I have to have another margarita?" I mumbled.

She didn't skip a stroke in brushing her hair in front of the mirror. She answered in a voice that was way too happy for the way I felt. "You might as well, honey. You know the first one is free."

Chapter 11

MORE THAN JUST PIE

The late afternoon sun streamed through the front door bathing the small waiting area in a soft glow. The blue vinyl bench which encircled the small room provided little comfort as I leaned back against the wall and quietly sipped my can of soda. I had never seen the place so empty.

The only other occupants were an older couple, probably late sixties, sitting a few feet away off to my left. The woman had on a long, blue print dress that hung down to her ankles. I studied her sharp facial features as she sat there quietly absorbed in a paperback book.

The man next to her was leaning back against the wall and staring straight ahead as if he were pondering something important. He was rather small and plumpish, with a round, pudgy face. His bright yellow shirt contrasted against his dark brown pants. A matching pair of large, brown suspenders clung to his slumping shoulders. And he had the inscrutably peculiar habit of twiddling his thumbs a mile a minute.

I had been to this restaurant before, many times. Sometimes on Sunday mornings after church, Diana and I would come in here for breakfast, or in the middle of the week we would come in here for dinner. Each time the place would be packed. Commotion would be everywhere. We would have to walk through a small group of people that would be standing outside waiting to be seated. Once inside, we would be met by a cacophony of noises – the tinkling of plates and glasses, cooks hollering out orders, and the gentle buzz of conversation.

On those occasions, the vinyl benches lining the small waiting area would almost always be full. A sea of hungry diners would look up at us as we would elbow our way over to the main desk and put our name on the waiting list. Then we would find a place to stand, out of the way, until a spot opened up for us to sit down. It was bedlam.

But on this particular visit, all was quiet. At 4:15 in the afternoon, the lunch crowd was long gone and the dinner rush was still an hour or so away. Soft casual conversation could be heard from the scattered diners in the dining area and a general mood of calmness permeated the air. The contrast to what I had always experienced in this place on other occasions was almost otherworldly.

I sat there quietly waiting, every so often discreetly glancing at the couple to my left and wondering why they were there. Seating certainly couldn't have been a problem this time of day as the dining area wasn't even half full. I shrugged my shoulders and took another sip of soda from the can in my right hand.

At least I knew why I was there and it wasn't to eat dinner either. I was running an errand; a common occurrence in my Arizona routine.

It had all started about fifteen minutes earlier. I'd been minding my own business at home, sitting on the sofa with my feet up, and fully engaged in reading the paper. I was really getting into it, too.

This had always been a cherished moment in my day, nestled deep in the cushions of the sofa, holding the newspaper up in front of me, the faint smell of fresh newsprint reaching my nostrils. I treasured the time I spent scanning the pages, searching for something interesting to read.

Suddenly, I was jolted out of my reading by the sound of Diana's urgent voice coming from somewhere in front of me.

"You know, we're going to need a pie for tonight."

My concentration on the printed words in front of me came to a crashing halt. Reluctantly, I looked up from the article I was reading and peered out over the top of the paper. There was the blur of Diana moving across the room as if she were being chased by a herd of buffalo.

I followed her with my eyes as she passed in front of me like a streak, disappearing through the sliding glass doors into the Arizona room.

Uh oh, I thought. Something was up. This was not a good sign. I got the feeling that my reading time was just about to wrap up. I gave my newspaper a good shake and tried to focus my eyes once again on the article that had my attention. I read another paragraph or two and was soon absorbed once again in the act of reading.

With a sudden clamor, Diana burst into the room for a second time. "Okay, come on. You're going to have to help me if we're having the Johnsons over for dessert."

The Johnsons? My mind tried to shift gears as I once again tore my eyes reluctantly from the page.

Diana was standing a few feet away from me, unwinding a cord on the vacuum cleaner. It took a few seconds of observation before I could fully comprehend the situation.

Oh, yes. The Johnsons, I thought. They were coming over tonight. I had forgotten all about it. Grudgingly, I folded the paper and laid it down on the coffee table. Reading time was now over.

"You have your choice," she said, as she grabbed the end of the cord on the vacuum cleaner. "You can either start vacuuming the house or you can go to the restaurant and get a pie." I watched as she pulled the cord over to an outlet in the wall with all the hustle of a firefighter dragging a hose to a burning building.

Let me see, I thought. I could either vacuum or go get a pie. Hmmm. I mulled these two choices over in my mind as I slowly rose from the sofa, stretching and yawning. I tried to make it appear as if it were a difficult decision for me, when in fact it was a no-brainer. What husband in his right mind would choose vacuuming over getting a pie?

"Oh, I don't know," I said. "I guess I could venture out into the traffic and get the pie." I tried to make it sound as though the slight apprehension in my voice made it appear as though I was volunteering for a dangerous mission.

"Well, okay", she said, easing the handle of the vacuum cleaner down with her right hand. "But hurry up. There is a lot of dusting to do as well."

I nodded and made a beeline for the door, grabbing a soda out of the fridge along the way. I wanted to get out of there as fast as possible.

"Oh, be sure to get a cream pie. Banana, coconut, something like that," Diana said loudly at my retreating back.

I smiled and waved as I grabbed the keys and disappeared into the garage. There wasn't any doubt what kind of pie I would get. When the choice is left up to me, it's banana cream every time. The vacuum cleaner started up with a roar as I closed the door behind me.

The restaurant was less than a five-minute drive away. We had gotten pies there a couple of other times before and we were always pleased with the result. It wasn't long before I was entering the front door and walking through the nearly deserted waiting area towards the glass display case that held the tempting pies.

A young woman who had short, dark curly hair and

wearing a brown apron, stood behind the counter. As I approached, she smiled and looked at me with a friendly expression on her face. "Hi. Can I help you?"

"I'd like to buy one of your pies," I said, setting my soda can down on top of the counter and rubbing my hands together. I gazed into the display case at the luscious cream pies.

"Okay, which one would you like?" she asked, bending over and opening the case.

"Do you have a banana cream?"

"Well, let's see." The young woman began lifting the edges of the pies gently with her fingertips. "This one's coconut cream, here's a chocolate cream." She bit her lip in concentration. "Another coconut cream." She lifted up the edge of the fourth one higher than the others. "And this one's...strawberry cream." She stood up and wiped her fingers on her apron. "Sorry, we don't seem to have a banana cream pie right now."

"Oh, that's too bad," I said, continuing to stare down at the pies. "I really had my heart set on banana cream." I was just about ready to choose a coconut cream, when the young woman spoke up, apparently sensing my disappointment.

"You know, there might be some more pies back in the kitchen. Why don't you have seat while I go check?"

The young woman hurried into the dining area and disappeared around a corner. I grabbed my can of soda and headed over to the padded bench.

The two people next to me were my only companions. I leaned back and took a sip. Every once in a while I would steal a glance over at the other couple. She still read her book, and he continued to twiddle his thumbs.

They were your typical snowbird couple, not unlike the tens of thousands of others who came to Arizona every winter. They seemed to be in no particular hurry and appeared unconcerned about anything as they sat there. But what were they doing there and what were they waiting for? Surely, they didn't have a pie coming, too?

Just then, the soft din of dining room conversation was interrupted by the sound of a door opening down a short hallway where the restrooms were located off to my right. Although it was impossible to look down that hallway from my position, it was apparent that someone was heading our way. The unmistakable creaking of the door and then the sound it made as it slammed closed filled the quiet waiting area like a tree falling in a forest.

I waited for the sound of footsteps, but for the longest time I heard nothing. My first reaction was to get up and look around the corner, but I resisted. I waited a few more seconds, waiting for some movement or breathing or coughing, anything that would prove that someone had just come out of the restroom. But still, no sound came from down the hall.

I looked over at the couple seated next to me. Certainly they, too, had heard the door opening and would be turning their heads in anticipation of someone approaching.

But they remained in the same pose they had been in since I had first sat down beside them. The lady was oblivious to her surroundings with her head buried in her paperback, the man leaning back against the wall, staring straight ahead, furiously twiddling his thumbs.

Just as I was beginning to wonder if my imagination had been playing tricks on me, I heard a faint rasping sound coming from down the hallway, as if someone had slowly begun dragging their feet across the floor. This rasping sound was accompanied by a rhythmic clump-clump. Rasp rasp-clump clump. Rasp rasp-clump clump. I sat up, my eyes riveted to the corner of the wall where the hallway entered the waiting area. Needless to say, my curiosity had certainly been piqued.

I waited anxiously for this apparition to appear. Whoever it was coming down the hall was walking agonizingly slow. Gradually, the rhythmic rasp rasp-clump clump got closer and closer, until I could see the person's shadow fall in front of us across the shiny, tile floor of the waiting area.

A walker slowly began appearing in front of me from out of the entrance of the hallway. Two aged, gnarled hands held onto its handles, slowly lifting it up, moving it forward a few inches, and putting it back down.

Soon, the bent form of a woman appeared. Considerably older than the couple seated next to me, she had short, snow-white hair, and wore a long, light-colored dress. Her face, although wrinkled with age, showed a fierce determination as she concentrated on manipulating her walker in front of her. Rasp rasp-clump clump. Rasp rasp-clump clump.

She made her way past me slowly and deliberately, not lifting her head to acknowledge the presence of anyone in the room, but rather keeping her concentration firmly on the walker and on her slow, rhythmic steps. Like something out of the old tale "The Tortoise and The Hare," she made her way ever so slowly across the waiting area. Rasp rasp-clump clump. Rasp rasp-clump clump.

I looked at the couple seated next to me, expecting to see them staring at the old woman, too. But they were not. The woman continued reading her book unperturbed; the man continued twiddling his thumbs. It was as if they were oblivious to the rest of their surroundings.

I sat there unable to keep my eyes off the old woman as she inched her way across the room. She was apparently headed for the door, intending to leave the restaurant and go outside into the parking lot. But how? Why? Surely she didn't drive here by herself.

When she reached the middle of the room, she suddenly stopped, her bent form resting on the handles of the walker.

Now standing directly in front of the thumb twiddler, she slowly turned her head and looked directly at him.

For the last few months, it had become a routine of mine to quite innocently watch these retired people in Arizona go through the motions of their daily lives. There was no escaping it, of course. It was all around me wherever I went – parks, shopping malls, restaurants. The locations would change, but the pattern would always be the same. Older, retired people making their way around the best they could.

I never really knew when one of these little melodramas would suddenly pop up before my eyes. They just did, and often quite unexpectedly. And although these occasions were not something I consciously sought out, I would watch with rapt attention nonetheless whenever one presented itself.

The woman with the walker, however, was an enigma. What was she doing there? It didn't make any sense. Obviously, she wasn't out on the town by herself, riding up and down the streets in her Corvette, enjoying the afternoon, and deciding on a whim to stop in and have a late lunch. Or was she? I leaned back on the blue vinyl bench and took one long, last sip on my can of soda, wondering what was going to happen next.

Abruptly, the man's thumbs stopped twirling round and round. He sat up as if coming out of a long slumber and put his hands on his knees. Looking at the woman, he jerked his thumb in the direction of the door.

"Well, Agnes," he said in a slow, halting voice. "You, uh, can start heading on out to the car now. We'll be along shortly."

The old woman looked at the man and nodded, and then resumed her slow, methodical walk towards the door. Rasp rasp-clump clump. Rasp rasp-clump clump.

At these words, my eyes widened in panic as my throat

suddenly attempted to expel the soda that I had been swallowing. My body involuntarily jerked forward as I was racked by a violent coughing attack. Had I heard him right? Was I dreaming? Not wanting to spit soda all over the room, I cupped my hand to my mouth and forced myself to swallow in between coughs. My lungs started burning as some of the soda apparently went down the wrong pipe.

I looked over at the old woman through red, burning eyes. Her frail body was slowly retreating away from me.

Rasp rasp-clump clump. Rasp rasp-clump clump.

The man had resumed his previous pose, leaning back against the bench and staring straight ahead, his thumbs twiddling round and round and round. The woman next to him remained totally absorbed in her reading. As far as I could tell, she'd never even lifted her head.

Cupping my hand to my mouth again, I stifled a couple of more coughs. I needed to get out of there for a minute to compose myself. I got up off of the bench and walked briskly down the hall and into the men's restroom. Once inside, I threw my empty soda can away and turned the cold water on in the sink. Staring into the mirror, I could see that my eyes were bloodshot from all the coughing.

Maybe I wasn't giving these people down here in Arizona enough credit, I thought. After all, they know what they're capable of doing more than I do. Nobody would make an old woman with a walker go out into a parking lot by herself, unless they knew she could do it; unless they knew everything was going to be all right. Would they?

Pondering this thought for a minute, I looked at my red rimmed eyes in the mirror and listened to the water run into the sink. I could only come up with one logical answer to my question. No, they wouldn't.

Or would they?

I chuckled to myself in the mirror and bent my head

down to the sink. Cupping my hands under the faucet I washed the cool water over my face several times. The wet sensation reinvigorated me, waking me up a little bit.

When I got back, the old woman and her walker were gone. She had presumably disappeared out the door and into the parking lot. How she managed to open that door and get through it with her walker, I had no clue. I'd missed that part of the show.

Impulsively, I headed for the door to see if she was okay. But then I stopped. The thumb twiddler didn't seem to be in any state of worry. He was still in his usual pose, as well as the woman next to him. I let out a sigh and sunk back down onto the bench.

Impatiently, I looked down to the other end of the dining area, the direction in which the young lady had left to see about my banana cream pie. It had been a while now since I had seen her last, and I began to wonder if she had forgotten about me. I didn't see her anywhere.

Suddenly the man stopped twiddling his thumbs. He sat up, putting his left hand on the woman's knee. "Well mother," he said with a huge sigh, looking over at the woman. "I suppose she should be pretty close to the car by now. We better get going."

The woman stopped reading, the first time I could recall seeing her lift her head. She looked over at the man, nodded, and closed her book.

Together, and with great difficulty, they stood up, joints popping, small groans issuing from their lips. They stood there for a few seconds gathering their balance. Then the man put his hand in the small of the woman's back and slowly began guiding her towards the door.

"Sir?"

I sat there transfixed, my mouth agape as these two now familiar figures disappeared out the door.

"Oh, sir, I have your pie ready to go. Sir?"

Somewhat startled, I looked over at the counter and there was the young woman who had waited on me earlier. She was smiling softly and holding an enormous cream-filled pie.

"I was able to find what you were looking for. A banana cream pie."

I stared at the woman for a second. A banana cream pie? "Oh, right, right," I said as I got up off the bench and walked over to the counter.

"You were in luck," she said as she gently lowered the mouth-watering delicacy into a box. "When I got back to the kitchen, it took a while to find the right cook," she said, closing the box and wiping her hands on her apron. She looked up at me with a smile. "But once I found him, he was able to direct me to just what you wanted. I hope you weren't bored with all the waiting."

I turned and looked at the door leading to the parking lot. There was not a soul to be seen.

"Oh no, no, I was fine," I said, nodding to the waiting area. "I had something to entertain myself."

Chapter 12

FEEDING THE BIRDS
TO THE BIRDS

I saw it out of the corner of my eye.

I was ten feet above the ground, inside the cab of our huge Case-IH tractor. Gently swaying back and forth in my seat as the tractor crawled slowly over the uneven field, I could hear the muffled roar of the diesel engine in the background. Instinctively, I looked in the direction of the sudden movement. Just ahead of me and off to the left, scurrying along the hard brown earth, was the plump gray form of a field mouse. He was frantically running away from the path of my tractor. Although this was a sight I had observed a million times in my life, it was also a cue. A signal that something riveting was about to happen.

It was late April and potato planting was in full swing. My job during this time of year was to till the fields, break up the top foot-and-a-half of soil. Just as a gardener prepares his plot with a rototiller, readying the soil for the planting of his corn or squash or beans, I too had to prepare the fields for our potato crop. It was the same principal exactly, only in my case, the scale was much larger, thousands of times larger, and the job would take weeks to complete.

Like clockwork, I would climb up into the tractor every

spring and pull the wide tiller through eleven hundred acres of ground, stirring up swaths of earth in my wake. This was an essential part of the planting process. A few days later, the potato planters would come along and mechanically drop the potato pieces into the soft, receptive soil. The breaking up of the earth, hardened by winter's frosty grip, was a pre-planting ritual that had been practiced every spring all over the world in one form or another for thousands of years.

It would be during this spring field work that I saw them, hundreds of them. In fact, if someone had given me a dime for every mouse I'd seen in my life, I would be a very, very rich man.

They lived a fat and sassy life these mice, all winter long in their vast network of tunnels, just a few inches under the ground. As long as they couldn't be seen, they were safe. But oh, did their fortunes change once the snow melted from the fields. Their peaceful existence would suddenly be shattered by the enormous equipment that would start rolling over the ground, tearing away their environment with ruthless abandon. Mice would be forced out of their safe tunnels and into the open for the first time, left to scurry away from the approaching danger like refugees running from a flood.

Ah, but to a bored tractor driver, this was great theater. Because, you see, mice that were running all around out there in the open were jumping from the frying pan and into the fire. Big fat mice, exposed out in the middle of a bare field, instantly became the main course of a sumptuous feast for the birds.

If there was one thing that stood out during the humdrum, monotonous day of driving a tractor on a farm, it was the birds, the constant presence of a cloud of noisy, hungry birds following along behind. After a long winter of scrounging around for food wherever they could find it, spring tilling was like Thanksgiving to them.

Every day, a huge flock of gulls would fly low behind my tractor, swooping down to consume the countless number of insects and worms that were being exposed in the freshly tilled soil. Squawking and crying as if they couldn't believe their good fortune, hundreds of these gray and white birds would spend large portions of the day loitering around in my vicinity. They were everywhere, gliding gracefully in the air behind my tractor or sitting on the ground off to the side, gorged full and resting as I chugged by.

Enter the poor field mouse, stage left. Often I would spot him from my tractor seat scampering along the ground. The little creature would zigzag this way and that, desperately trying to find some cover, when all of a sudden he would be spotted from above. Half a dozen or more gulls would swoop down on him like fire engines arriving at a fire. They would trot around him with their wings spread, squawking, pecking at him with their large orange beaks, toying with the terrified mouse. Finally, a gull would have had enough of this play and he would snatch the mouse up with his beak and fly off, swallowing the poor hapless mouse in flight with other gulls following in pursuit.

This scenario had played out before my tractor driving eyes countless number of times over the years. And yet, like a motorist slowing down to gawk at a wreck, I couldn't keep my eyes off of it. It was real. It was raw. It was survival of the fittest in its most natural form and I sat and watched it from seat of my Case IH every spring.

And so, it was against this backdrop that I watched that mouse scurry around on the ground on that cool April day.

From my vantage point, the mouse looked like a grey, furry dot scrambling along the dirt, its little legs churning a mile a minute. Little did the poor fellow know that it was only seconds away from becoming some seagull's lunch.

As the tractor moved forward, I watched and waited, expecting the gulls to swoop down and surround their prey any second. But the seconds ticked by. The mouse continued to run aimlessly across the open field. And although I could see them in my rearview mirror, gliding in the air behind me, for some reason, the gulls weren't coming.

Then unexpectedly, I was startled by a large, dark form hurtling towards the ground. It dove past my window in a lightning quick blur. It was so big and traveling so fast, that it was if a bowling ball had been dropped from the sky next to my tractor. My heart jumped up in my throat by the suddenness of it, and I watched as this dark, moving mass quickly landed on the mouse.

It was a hawk, a large magnificent hawk that I had seen from time to time out in the fields. It stood there for a few seconds, very straight and erect, with the mouse in its talons on the ground. He turned his head from side to side, looking around with its curved beak pointing to the ground. And then, just as suddenly as he'd appeared, he took off. As the tractor continued on, the hawk slowly spread its huge wings and rose up from the ground with the mouse in its grasp. With its wide wings gently waving up and down, the hawk glided effortlessly past my front window, its neck stretched out and its sleek head pointing forward. It was an awesome sight to see. He flew off to the east and disappeared from my view.

The day continued on, uneventful. Hours went by as I pulled the tiller back and forth through the field, dust rising up in the air behind me, the engine droning on. But as I drove, no matter where my thoughts would drift, my mind would come back to that hawk. I couldn't stop thinking how he had so suddenly come upon the scene and how the seagulls had seemingly given deference to him as if he were some kind of king of the field. But most of all, I couldn't help but be reminded of a similar event that had happened a few months earlier back in Arizona.

It was the middle of February and I was lying back in my lounge chair enjoying the afternoon warmth of our back patio. My hands were folded behind my head as a soft breeze rattled the newspapers that were sitting in my lap. My gaze was riveted to the Superstition Mountains in the east.

Oh, how I love to sit and stare at those mountains. Like a battleship sailing on a calm sea, the Superstitions rose up off of the flat desert floor, stretching north to south against the backdrop of a cobalt blue Arizona sky. It was mesmerizing to look at them. And on lazy afternoons, I would often do just that.

Sometimes, my eyes would be pulled away from my paper by a sudden furious movement in front of me. Instinctively, I would look up over the top of my paper and see nothing but our rose bushes lining the edge our patio. Then like a mirage appearing from out of nowhere, I would see several small, finches perched in them not far from my chair.

They were inquisitive little things, and I loved to watch them whenever they showed up. Small enough that I could have held one in the palm of my hand, the finches were constantly looking around them as if on a frenetic search. They would look up, then down, then side to side, always turning their heads in quick, robot-like movements. But they never stayed long on their perch. Just a few seconds or so, long enough for me to just start getting a good look at them. Then they would suddenly dart away again, taking flight out of my view as quickly as they had arrived.

Sometimes I would be reading my paper and happen to look up and see a family of Gambel's Quail strutting by on the grass. These noble looking birds, with their large plumes rising up over their heads, would slowly parade past the back of our house, pecking at the ground here and there and acting like they hadn't a care in the world.

I must say that the Gambel's Quail and the little finches were a frequent source of amusement for me during my visits to our patio. But the king of the realm, the undisputed monarch of the bird kingdom in our area, was the huge hawk that seemed to have adopted our park as its personal domain. He was a mysterious and elusive figure, seen only on the rarest of occasions. But when this magnificent bird saw fit to make an appearance, his imposing size and his dignified demeanor left no doubt as to who ruled.

There would be times when I would step through the sliding glass doors onto our patio and there would be the hawk off in the distance. He would be sitting in a tree or some other lonely perch, quietly holding his head up high and staring straight ahead, sometimes for hours at a time, surveying his realm. He cast an even more ominous presence through my binoculars; dark brown feathers with streaks of white on his chest, long talons clamping down on his perch like a vise, his curved beak accentuating his already daunting profile.

He would sit there for hours, perfectly still, staring straight ahead. Then without warning he would leave. The hawk would suddenly leap from his perch like an uncoiled spring, his eight-foot wingspan casting a shadow on the green grass below. With his neck outstretched, the large hawk would slowly gain altitude with his wings flapping up and down, smoothly, effortlessly.

The hawk's large body would gradually rise up into the air. Soaring above the houses of our park, he would slowly disappear into the Arizona sky, not to be seen again for a week, perhaps two.

One day, when both Diana and I were out on the patio relaxing and watching the little birds come and go on our rosebushes, we got the bright idea that we should get a bird feeder. We felt it would give us a chance to watch these little creatures more closely, while at the same time give them something to eat. The more we talked about it, the more we liked the idea. Soon we were in our car, wending our way to Wal-Mart and beginning, what we hoped would be our small contribution to the natural habitat of Arizona's desert environment.

It wasn't more than an hour later that I found myself standing next to our patio table gazing down at a contraption that, until that day, I had never seen before. It was a clear plastic tube a foot-and-a-half long and about six inches in diameter. The directions were pretty straightforward. After fumbling with the various parts and gazing back and forth between the diagram and the bird feeder, I had managed to piece the thing together. Standing back, looking at the finished product, I admired my handiwork.

The long slender cylinder had four holes cut in its side, two at the bottom and another two in the middle. Under each hole were the perches, two-inch long metal rods sticking out from the tube.

I looked at the ten-pound bag of bird seed that was resting next to it. "Gourmet Wild Bird Feed" the package read in bright red lettering across the top. The bag was bursting with all kinds of colorful seeds – black sunflower seeds, golden wheat, red safflower seeds, and on and on. The list of ingredients ended with the words "added nutrients, vitamins and minerals for birds." Well, I thought, if nothing else, the little finches that came around our place were going to be the healthiest birds in Arizona. I hung the bird feeder from the crook of a tall shepherd's pole that we had used to hang a pot of flowers on.

For the next two days, nothing happened. My patio time would be spent reading the paper and waiting, waiting for some birds to help themselves to our treat. Every few minutes, I'd sneak a look at the bird feeder, but there would be nothing there. It had seemed as if our new acquisition wasn't working.

I was just beginning to think that the bird feeder was a big flop when, on the third day, I happened to peek around my newspaper and see two little birds sitting on the perches and sticking their heads inside the tube. I apparently moved too quickly in putting down my paper to get a better look. In an instant, the tiny creatures flitted away and disappeared, leaving me staring at the vacant bird feeder that was slowly swaying a few inches back and forth on the end of the shepherd's pole. I had scared them away.

I picked up my paper again and waited quietly, patiently. The patio was not just a patio anymore. I was sitting in a blind for birds and the newspaper had become my cover. But now I was bungling it all up. I desperately wanted some birds to land on that bird feeder. It had become my all-consuming passion. But now I was scaring them away.

My patience was rewarded only a couple of minutes later when, after breaking away from reading the same sentence for the umpteenth time, I saw that the little birds had reappeared.

I held my breath. You could have clocked geologic time with the slowness with which I brought my newspaper down into my lap. I sat perfectly still, spellbound by what I was seeing.

I guess I had always taken birds for granted. Back home of course, I saw them all the time. Not only the gulls, ravens, and hawks that would keep me company out in the fields, but others as well.

I had seen hundreds of sparrows perched in a straight line on a telephone wire as if they were waiting for some momentous thing to happen. And as I would draw closer to them in my pickup, they would all rise as one, ascending up into the air in a heaving, dark cloud and drift across the sky.

I had even seen huge pelicans down by the reservoir, floating on the water and feeding on the fish that ventured too close to the surface.

I had seen flocks of Canada geese gliding over our house on brisk autumn mornings, honking feverishly as they flew in their huge, v-shaped formations.

Yes, the presence of birds had been forever interwoven into my everyday life. But they had always been just on the edge of my awareness. I never really had the interest to take a serious hard look at them. Until now!

When those two small finches finally landed on our bird feeder and started feeding on the seeds, it opened up the floodgates. The next few days saw a beehive of activity. Hardly a minute would go by without a least two or three birds sitting on the perches, clinging to the shiny metal and retrieving the seeds from within. Sometimes, the same birds would sit there for ten minutes or more, completely oblivious to my presence just a few feet away, as they feasted on the colorful seeds.

This provided me with a rare opportunity to enter a world that had been unimaginable to me just a few days earlier. I became enamored with the tiny creatures and found myself gawking at them for long periods of time.

Through my 7×35 binoculars, I could easily see the different shadings of color and tone that varied from bird to bird. The finches with their red-tinged shoulders and heads, the swallows with their creamy grey sleek bodies, and the sparrows with their gray coloring accentuated by dark streaks slashed across their faces and necks. I was struck by their delicate appearance, the intricacy of their perfectly proportioned bodies and their timid and inquisitive personalities.

Before now they had been…well…just birds, not worth thinking about really. But from this perspective, they now had become unique living beings. Over the coming days, I came to respect them, acknowledging that we all shared the same place in time and space. Watching them humbled me.

But that was all about to change.

Over the course of the next few days, the activity around our back patio increased markedly. While the bird feeder only had room for four little birds to perch on at a time, the demand for those four perches soon far exceeded supply. Word must have gotten out pretty fast in the East Valley about the free buffet at our park. The foliage bordering our back patio gradually became filled with a noisy, black cloud, a waiting room for the ever-increasing flock of customers.

To make matters worse, a new set of clientele had entered the fray, grayish-white doves, birds that I had never seen around before. They appeared one day to join in the banquet. Being too large to sit on the little perches, the doves busied themselves by strutting around the bottom of the shepherd's pole, kicking rocks away with their feet and pecking at the ground for the seeds that were being dropped from above.

It wasn't long before the quiet time out on the patio with my newspaper had become a chirping, twittering, wing-flapping, bird-pooping nightmare.

Then one morning, I was standing at the sink in the bathroom, brushing my teeth, when I heard this muffled, bloodcurdling scream emanating from the Arizona room in the back of the house. Startled out of my wits, I dropped my toothbrush and ran to the source of the god-awful scream, wiping toothpaste off of my mouth with my pajama sleeve as I ran. When I entered the Arizona room, Diana was standing at the sliding glass doors.

She turned and looked at me. Her face was pale and she was visibly upset. "We're setting a trap for the doves," she said with a quiver in her voice. "We're accessories to murder."

What on earth? I stepped up to the glass and peered through the winged commotion that had become our patio. There on the branch of a tree not twenty yards away sat the hawk. He was in the middle of breakfast, ripping apart a dove with his beak. The hapless little dove had become his prey. I watched with my mouth open as his huge beak ripped at the lifeless body clenched between the sharp talons. White feathers slowly drifted down from the branch to the bright green lawn below.

∞

A warm breeze drifted over me and stirred the newspaper lying in my lap. The sun was bright and the afternoon was clear. I sat in the lounge chair and looked out at the Superstition Mountains which dominated the eastern horizon. I turned my head slightly to the left and looked at the shepherd's pole. A pot of brilliant red and white petunias dangled from the end.

It had been almost a year since the bird feeder episode, and the patio was now once again a peaceful place. Two small finches suddenly flew into my line of sight. For a brief moment, they sat on a nearby palm branch, turning their small heads this way and that. Then in an instant, they took flight again and disappeared into the sky.

A fleeting thought entered my mind. Maybe we should try the bird feeder again. After all, they were cute.

I inexplicably visualized in my mind's eye a scene from

Alfred Hitchcock's movie *The Birds*. In my vision, I saw Tippi Hedren running down a road with thousands of blackbirds screeching and flying after her. They began pecking at her sweater, pecking at her hair. I shuddered in my lounge chair and immediately made up my mind.

No! The bird feeder is doing just fine where it is, taking up space in the garage.

Chapter 13

HOPE BLOOMS ETERNAL
AT SPRING TRAINING

I could hardly believe my eyes. There, just a few steps from home plate, sprawled out on the ground in obvious pain, was Nomar Garciaparra, the star shortstop for the Chicago Cubs. He'd swung at a slider down and away and grounded it to short, taken a step or two towards first base and then had crumpled to the ground. It was awful to watch.

Coaches and trainers rushed to his side and knelt over him as he rolled around on the dirt, both of his hands clutching his groin, his face twisted in pain. After a few minutes, Nomar was carried off the field in a sitting position by two trainers and disappeared into the dugout and down the tunnel leading to the clubhouse.

I stared at the TV in stunned silence. It was April 20th, 2005, a cool spring evening in southeast Idaho. Rain had sent me home early from the day's tilling out in the field. As was my custom, I was dutifully stationed at my resting spot in front of the TV watching baseball. Tonight, it was the Cubs playing the Cardinals at Busch Stadium in St. Louis, a bitter interdivisional rivalry. It had been a while since I had last checked in on the Cubbies, and I was anxious to see how they were doing.

Being only three weeks removed from following the Cubs spring training in Mesa, I was inexorably entwined with their fortunes. Hohokam Park, the Chicago Cubs spring training facility, is only a short ten-minute drive from our home in Mesa. Over the years, I had spent many a March afternoon drinking beer and munching on hot dogs while watching the lovable losers from the north side of Chicago perform on the bright green grass of Hohokam.

This was to be a pivotal year for the Cubs. Their long-suffering fans were still waiting for the team's first World Series title since 1908, but this year (once again) they had renewed hope. The previous fall, the baseball Gods had looked down and saw fit to lift the curse of the Bambino, giving the Boston Red Sox the title for the first time since 1918. The lifting of a curse had to be a good omen for the Cubs as well.

During last season, the Cubs had traded for a real superstar at shortstop. Nomar Garciaparra had been a fixture in a Boston Red Sox uniform for many years. With a couple of batting titles to his credit, Nomar brought hope to the Cubs faithful that he would increase the team's chances of getting to the World Series. As spring training approached, there was a lot of optimism for 2005 on the north side of Chicago.

But if the Cubs were to be winners, much was expected from their new star. Having just dealt away their aging but longtime premier player Sammy Sosa to Baltimore, much of the Cub's offense was riding on Nomar's shoulders.

And he had just finished having a monster spring, hitting homer after homer and driving in runs by the bushel. Nomar indeed seemed poised and ready to take over the new leadership role on the club.

So, when I read a few days later that the injury was very serious, muscle tearing away from bone, and that Nomar would miss most of the rest of the year, I was haunted by an incident that happened about a month before. I was haunted by the words of one Bill Casey.

The saga of Bill Casey began for me one February morning a few months earlier while I was on a treadmill in the exercise room at our park in Arizona. This room had become somewhat of a sanctuary for me since I had arrived in Arizona the previous fall. Reluctantly, I had somehow coaxed myself into spending forty minutes a day on the treadmill and after a while, was surprised to find myself welcoming this daily routine. I looked forward to meeting new people there and listening to their stories as they labored beside me.

This particular day was no different. There I was toiling away, walking my usual pace with my hands clutching the rails on the side. I was working up a sweat, marching along step after step. I was doing my best to accommodate Dr. Mansfield back home, who had assured me that such a daily workout would guarantee me a long and healthy life. No one else was in the room at the moment. My sneakers clomped along through the background noise of the T V set that was up on a wall in front of me.

Suddenly, the serenity of the moment was disturbed by the sound of the door to the exercise room opening. A man in his mid-seventies entered the room. I couldn't remember ever seeing him before. He had thick, gray hair and sported a small gray goatee. He was certainly decked out for the occasion, wearing shorts and a T-shirt. He nodded and smiled at me as he got up on the treadmill next to mine and wordlessly started walking at a moderate pace. I continued to march along as the whirr of the treadmills droned on.

After a short time, the man stuck a meaty hand in my chest and with a loud commanding voice announced, "Bill Casey here. Pleased to make your acquaintance."

I noticed he had a slight accent, but couldn't immediately

place it. Without missing a step, I wiped the sweat from my right hand on my shirt and shook his hand. "Len Schritter here," I said, trying to smile through the physical exertion that I was expending.

"I'm from Ireland," he blurted out. "Came over here when I was just a young lad. Yep. Irish through and through."

An awkward silence fell between us for a few seconds and the only sound in the room was the TV and the constant whirring of our two machines with our footsteps pounding away.

I felt obliged to tell him where I was from and opened my mouth to do so. "Well, I'm from…" I started to say.

"Yep, Ireland's where I was born and raised," said the man next to me, oblivious to my attempt to join in the conversation. "Only twenty when I arrived on these shores. I lived in Boston for many years. Just moved here last summer."

He said this looking straight ahead while he plied the treadmill. For a moment, it was hard to tell if he was directing his words at me or just daydreaming out loud. I waited before I spoke, wanting to make sure that he was done talking before I offered my two cents worth. When I thought it was finally safe to speak, I said, "Well, I'm from Idaho, and I…"

"Idaho," he interrupted. "They grow lots of potatoes there, don't they? Ireland had a real bad potato famine many a year ago. Maybe you heard of it. Lots of my countryman starved to death. Oh, my!" He shook his head sadly. "I tell you, 'twas a hard time back then, a hard time."

He had spoken with such passion and conviction that it seemed as if he had personally lived through this sad piece history himself. I could see he was now lost in thought as a long silence again fell between us, intermingled with the sound of the newscast on TV and our heavy footsteps on the treadmills.

However, I was undaunted. The topic of the Irish potato famine had sparked my interest, and I felt now that I had something important to say. I knew though that once I opened my mouth, I had better be quick. I took a deep breath and dove in.

"Well, Bill, the Irish potato famine was caused by something called late blight. You don't have to worry about that anymore. That can all be controlled by crop dusting now days." The words rattled off my tongue as fast as I could form them.

I peeked over at him as he walked next to me and was surprised that I still had the floor.

"I know," I continued, "because I'm a potato farmer myself back in Idaho."

I stopped speaking and gasped deeply for air as if I had just come up from being underwater for a long time.

The man's head jerked around in my direction like he had suddenly just noticed that I was there. "My gawd! You're a potato farmer, you say?" His eyes then glazed over as if he were conjuring up memories of a long ago time.

"My dad was a potato farmer, too," he said. "Oh, the work me and my brothers and sisters had to do growing up in Ireland. Out all day in the fields, picking potatoes by hand, putting them in sacks. Backbreaking work, I tell ya. Why I could hardly stand up straight at the end of the day."

"Well, it's nothing like that today," I said. I was on a roll now. "They got machines to do all that. Tractors, trucks, harvesters, conveyer belts. Very little manual labor involved now days."

He looked over at me. Both of us still marching on the treadmills, our feet clomping along loudly. "I would love to see that," he said with an air of wonder in his voice. "By gawd, I would love to see something like that!"

We talked for several minutes as we continued exercising

together. He told me of his many grown sons scattered throughout the United States, about his being a widower for over twenty years and never remarrying. He told me about his recent retirement from a job in sales that had taken him all over the country. And he talked proudly of the fact that he was a Red Sox fan.

For the next several weeks, I saw Bill occasionally on the streets of our park. His face would light up the second he saw me and he would hurry over and tell me in great detail, with his touch of Irish brogue, "I told my neighbor…" Or, "I just told the cable man…" Or, "I just told old so and so that I know a real live potato farmer from Idaho."

Bill Casey was starting to make me feel like a genuine novelty.

As I mentioned, baseball was a big part of my life. Following the pennant races, the personal records being broken, and watching the playoffs and World Series were always highlights of my year.

It was only natural then that once we started coming to Arizona for the winter, I'd spend a lot of my time going to spring training games in the month of March. Diana was a willing participant in this endeavor. We would crisscross the Valley while I dragged her to stadium after stadium, sometimes attending two or three games a week.

Most of the time, she was as big a fan as I was, enjoying every hit, every strikeout, every double play. But chasing twelve major league teams around Arizona's Cactus League schedule is an arduous task that can test the mettle of even the most ardent baseball fan. Then, one day the inevitable happened. Diana had had enough. She said she needed a breather and was begging off from attending the next game on our list.

I opened my desk drawer and looked at the two tickets for tomorrow's game, the Cubs and the Brewers at Hohokam

Park, two seats just a few rows in from the playing field and down the right field line.

I hated to think of going to one of these games by myself, especially since I had paid for two tickets. And like a lot of things, baseball was more enjoyable if you could share the experience with someone else.

I hadn't the foggiest idea who I could get to go with me. Then the face of Bill Casey began forming in my mind. He seemed like the logical choice. I winced, however, at the possibilities. Here, in the safety of our retirement park, I always had the option of cutting short a conversation with the long-winded Irishman. I could always make an excuse and walk away. But seated next to him at a ball game? I could be setting myself up to be his personal captured audience. Oh well, I thought. Maybe the action on the field will keep him occupied.

Hohokam Park sits as a jewel not too far from downtown Mesa. To the Chicago Cub faithful, this small 12,000-seat baseball park tucked away among the retirement villas and condominiums in the lush surrounding community represents the culmination of an annual pilgrimage. Every year, thousands of Chicagoans plan their vacations around the Cubs spring training schedule, hopping on a plane and escaping the frozen shores of Lake Michigan in favor of the warmth of a bleacher seat in the Arizona sun.

Bill and I made our way slowly up the street in my car to the entrance of the stadium in the heavy game day congestion. As we crawled along in bumper-to-bumper traffic, we could see ticket scalpers and other merchandise hawkers standing on the curb displaying their wares as we went by.

"Boy, what a treat. I'm sure glad you asked me to come with ya," said Bill. "This is going to be great. And getting to see Nomar Garciaparra, a former Red Sox player, is going to be awesome. I sure hope he doesn't get injured."

"Why do you say that?" I demanded to know.

"Aw, jeez, he's always going down with an injury of some sort. I should know. I seen it many a time in Boston, ya know. Oh, he's a great player and all that…but oh those injuries. Ya just can't count on him."

I turned the steering wheel and we followed the line of cars into the front gates of the grounds. I handed the parking attendant a five dollar bill. Hohokam Park loomed over us off to our left. Its bright green façade and the colorful banners hanging from its rooftops were as alluring as the sight of presents underneath a Christmas tree. No matter how many times I had been to a spring training game, this feeling never changed. I didn't know how Bill felt, but I couldn't wait to get inside.

I parked the car, and Bill and I gathered up our stadium seat cushions, tickets, binoculars, bottles of frozen water, all the essential elements for enjoying an afternoon under the sun at Hohokam. As we joined the gathering parade of fans slowly walking towards the stadium, a sense of joyful anticipation sliced through the air.

Everyone was dressed for the occasion, wearing various forms of Cub garb. I was festooned, of course, in full team regalia. A blue T-shirt with the large Chicago Cub insignia plastered prominently on the front hung down to my bare knees. On my head sat a blue baseball cap with the familiar red "c" on the front. I had dressed for the occasion, as always, with great formality, standing in front of the mirror, appraising each new addition to my attire, not leaving for the game until I looked just right.

"Man!" Bill said, gazing up at the stadium with wide-eyed amazement. "I didn't know this was such a big deal. I was expecting something on a little smaller scale." He looked around at the people walking beside us. "Seems to be a pretty popular place."

"This is a big deal here, Bill." We had stopped walking and joined a line of people waiting to get through the turnstiles. "The Cubs are the biggest draw in the Cactus League."

The man at the entrance smiled broadly as he took our tickets and tore off the stubs. "Enjoy the game!" We entered the cool shade beneath the stadium and made our way through the clamor of arriving fans towards the tunnel.

As we came out the other side, the mint green grass of the diamond shimmered before us in the bright sunlight. I stood there for a moment soaking it all in. The pearl blue sky served as the perfect backdrop for the distant red mountains. The huge green wall in center field, the rich brown earth of the infield dirt, the sound of baseballs slapping into mitts, all of these things were intoxicating. They reminded me for the millionth time why I come to these games.

"This is really something!" Bill said distantly. He was gawking around the stadium. I could tell he was pleased and was enjoying the experience. And the game hadn't even started yet. "Once again, thank you for bringing me." He smiled at me, the corners of his eyes crinkling in the sunshine. "This is more than I expected."

We made our way to our section just down the third base line a few rows in and settled into our seats. A few minutes later, some of the gathering crowd in our area stood up and began cheering and applauding. When I looked to see what the ruckus was about, I noticed three Cub players had just emerged from the dugout and were slowly jogging towards us. Their toothpaste-white uniforms were blinding against the bright green grass. As they got closer, I could make out the detail of their pale blue pinstripes and the brilliant red "c" emblazoned on their chests. They smiled and waved to the crowd as they got closer, looking like they had just stepped out of the pages of *Sports Illustrated*."

"Hey, Nomar!" Bill hollered as he stood and clapped his hands enthusiastically, joining the rest of the fans in our area. "Knock 'em dead today, Nomar."

I recognized them instantly – Derrek Lee, Jeromy Burnitz, and Nomar Garciaparra. They stopped just in front of our seats, no more than thirty feet away, and began stretching and bending. Slowly, the cheering faded and the people began sitting back down in their seats, turning their attention once again back to their beers and their hot dogs and their programs.

"Ah, the great Nomar," Bill said softly as he sat back down, adjusting his cap with a few tugs on the bill. "What a great player he is." He stared wistfully at the three players as they continued to stretch and contort themselves at odd angles. "Tis a shame he's usually always hurt." He shook his head in dismay. "Any Red Sox fan could tell ya that it would be next to a miracle for him to put together a full season in good health."

Soon the stadium was full and the game got underway. Bill and I were content to sit under the sun-splashed sky and watch the action. We took turns getting hot dogs and beers. We concentrated on each foul ball that came our way, not getting any, by the way. And we joined in with the rest of the crowd in cheering for the Cubs. Bill kept his usual nonstop chatter surprisingly to a minimum. He seemed to be enjoying his first experience at Hohokam.

In the seventh inning, Garciaparra came up to the plate with the bases empty. He had already driven in a pair of runs with a double earlier in the game.

The buzz from the crowd started growing slowly as he strolled up to home plate carrying his bat. He pushed down on the top of his blue batting helmet with the palm of his hand. When he reached the edge of the batter's box, he took a few practice swings as his name was being announced over the loudspeakers amid the applause and cheers of the huge crowd.

I recognized the familiar ritual that Nomar went through at the batter's box. Before every pitch, he would step out and fiddle with his gloves, making his fingers look as if they were doing some rhythmical dance on top of his wrist. I had seen this familiar gesture dozens of times on TV and knew it by heart. (Pitch, step out, stand straight up, weight resting on the back foot, fingers instinctively tugging at his batting gloves, step back in.) The movements were almost robotic. The catcher, pitcher, and umpire had no choice but to wait patiently after each pitch for him to go through this routine.

He settled back into the batter's box and stared out at the pitcher. With a loud crack of the bat, Nomar connected on the next pitch. The crowd rose as one in full-throated roar. I stood and watched as the baseball soared high into the blue Arizona sky and landed into the colorful, sun-drenched crowd occupying the grassy berm beyond the left centerfield fence.

The Hohokam multitude roared its approval as Garciaparra trotted around the bases. He stepped on home plate amid raucous cheering and arrived at the dugout to be greeted by a happy gathering of his teammates. The fans stayed on their feet a long time and continued cheering for their hero.

None more so than Bill Casey.

"That's the way, Nomar. Way to go!" Bill yelled as he clapped enthusiastically. "Way to show 'em!" he shouted through cupped hands. "Yay, Nomar! What a hit." Bill was clapping so hard that I was afraid he might hurt his hands. His smile stretched from ear to ear, spreading his grey goatee across his chin. He was certainly lost in the moment.

As the cheering subsided, the crowd slowly sank back into their seats.

"What a player," Bill said shaking his head slowly over the buzz of the crowd. He picked up his beer next to his seat and took a sip. "Nomar can play with the best of 'em."

The sharp sound of the crack of the bat from the next batter echoed over the crowd as a foul ball was lofted back behind home plate. The crowd oohed and ahhed as the ball bounced high off the concrete floor and landed in the outstretched hands of a young fan wearing a Cub T-shirt.

"Ahh, but something will happen to him. It always does," Bill said matter-of-factly. He set his beer down by his seat and leaned back thoughtfully, his arms folded across his chest as he watched the action at home plate.

The sound of the baseball slapping hard into the catcher's mitt echoed throughout the stadium once again as the batter took a pitch.

"Maybe this will be Nomar's year," I said, grasping at straws in his defense. "Maybe he'll go through the whole year without getting hurt."

"Maybe," Bill said, shrugging his shoulders while still staring at the action at home plate. Then he turned to me and looked me in the eyes with a haggard face. "But I wouldn't hold my breath."

The words hung in the air like an icicle.

The pitcher peered in for his sign, wound up, and flung another pitch towards home plate. The batter swung and sent the ball careening in our direction. Bill and I ducked as it sailed over our heads and ricocheted off a railing some twenty feet behind us. I sat back up and took another sip of my beer, no worse for the wear.

I looked at the people around me in the stands. They were happy. With their Cub hats sitting on their heads and wearing their Chicago shirts and jerseys, they exuded sheer joyfulness. It was spring training after all. It was a time for optimism.

And yet, I was afraid. Ecstatic optimism is a dangerous mood to be in for Chicago Cub fans. By August, their smiles usually turn into scowls as their beloved Cubs once again squander away another season. And these fans I saw seated around me deserved better than that.

The Cubs hadn't won a World Series since 1908. *1908!* I thought of all the Cub greats who played in Wrigley Field summer after summer and never got the opportunity to play on baseball's biggest stage: Billy Williams, Ron Santo, Ferguson Jenkins, Ryne Sandberg, and Mr. Cub himself, Ernie Banks. Why, if you dwelt on it for very long, it could bring you to tears.

Gazing out at the bright green grass, sitting there amid the buzz of the crowd on that sunny March afternoon, I made a silent vow. I would become a Garciaparra fan. I would root for him throughout the summer from my recliner in Idaho. I would pull for Nomar to not only make it through the year without getting hurt, but to lead the Cubs to a pennant and to propel them into the World Series.

And I would show Bill Casey that he was wrong. It was the least I could do.

∞

As it turned out, Nomar Garciaparra came back from his injury in August and turned in an uneventful performance the rest of the season for the Cubs. In the off-season, he signed as a free agent with the Los Angeles Dodgers. That next season, the Dodgers made the playoffs and faced off with the Mets in the first round, where an injured Nomar spent most of the time watching helplessly from the dugout as his new team was swept in three games.

And the Cubs? Sadly, as of this writing in the spring of 2007, the Chicago Cubs were still looking for their first World Series victory since Teddy Roosevelt was president.

Chapter 14

GOING HOME

April always came fast in Arizona. Every spring, it seemed as though we'd just arrived, wide-eyed and excited with the promise of escaping from another frozen tomorrow. Then, before we knew it, we were packing up and getting ready to head back home again. Where had all the time gone?

I had been fitfully watching this day approach on the calendar for many weeks. Early April seemed so far away just a month or so ago. There had been so much to look forward to in these final weeks with the excitement of spring training, the promise of longer and warmer days, twilight dips in the pool. As each day melted into the next, time ceased to be relevant. The waning days of yet another snowbird season seemed to race across the March calendar in a wild blur of memorable moments.

And then it was over.

I tossed a pair of rolled up socks into the bottom of my suitcase and then peeked out our window. The light outside was quickly fading into an early April sunset, and a few lingering clouds in the east were tinged in red. The days were getting longer, which meant the desert would soon be in full bloom with all its vibrant colors. I turned and walked broodingly back to the dresser for another pair of socks. I really wasn't into this.

Tomorrow morning, we would be gone, joining the fast-growing exodus of winter visitors. People all over the park were pulling out for the summer. Everyday you could see a loaded-down van or car with license plates from North Dakota, Minnesota, Iowa, Canada, and all points beyond heading out the gate. Tomorrow, I would be squeezing my ample paunch, expanded by several weeks of spring training hot dogs and beer, behind the wheel of our car and once again heading back home. Tomorrow it would be our turn.

Suddenly, Diana entered the room in a rush, her arms loaded with warm clothes she'd just pulled out of the dryer. "Don't forget to pack those new shirts you bought down here. You'll need them back home."

I watched as she hurried past me and disappeared into the walk-in closet. "I won't," I mumbled, standing there eyeing the dresser drawer.

"And don't forget to go down to the office tomorrow morning before we leave and fill out the departure form." Diana appeared from the closet again. This time she was empty-handed as she brushed past me and disappeared into the living room.

"I won't," I reassured her.

I looked at the open dresser drawer a few feet in front of me. My mind was telling me to reach in there pull out something, anything, and then walk over and put it in the suitcase. But my body was telling me something different. I felt like I was standing underwater, unable to move very fast. Packing to go home should be something that was done with a little bit more purpose, a little bit more life. I should have been really getting into it, hurrying the process along. But the only thing I could think of was: Turn out the lights. The party's over.

Diana reentered the room with another armful of clothes and quickly disappeared into the closet. A few seconds later she appeared again in a rush. She took a couple of steps forward into the bedroom and then came to a sudden halt when she looked over at me.

"What are you doing just standing there? "We have a lot to get done tonight."

"I know," I said, staring at the dresser.

"Well…are you going to do something? Maybe move just a little bit?"

I looked at her impassively.

She put her hands on her hips. An awkward silence fell between us as we stared at each other for a few seconds. Then, a hint of recognition crossed her face.

"Come here" she said softly. I watched as she slowly walked over to the edge of the bed and sat down.

"Come over here and sit down by me." She patted the edge of the bed next to her and beckoned me with her soft, expectant eyes.

I turned and looked at her. She smiled up at me and patted the bed again, gesturing me to join her.

Slowly, I walked over to her and sat down. She put her arm around me and looked deep into my eyes. "Are you upset because we're leaving tomorrow?"

I looked at her for several seconds, unwilling to admit it, unwilling to admit that she could read me like a book.

"Kind of dumb, isn't it?"

"Oh, not at all," she replied, her eyes still riveted on mine. "That is a completely understandable feeling." She nodded her head and smiled. "In fact, I don't really want to leave too badly myself."

A siren could be heard in the distance, a common sound around the outside of our park. We both sat there for a moment without speaking, her arm around my shoulders.

"But we have to go back," she continued. "That's our home. That's where everything is that means anything to us. Our families, our grandkids, the farm…our house."

"I know, I know. But there's something you don't understand, something I really haven't talked much about that you should probably know."

"Oh my god. Don't tell me you're having an affair with one of these old ladies in here." She pulled her arm off my shoulders.

"No, no, are you crazy? That's not it."

"Well, what it is then?"

I folded my hands and looked into my lap. "Well, it's kind of silly but…"

"What?"

"It goes back to along time ago." I turned to look at her. "Farming wasn't what I really wanted to do with my life. But it was just kind of…expected."

"Expected?"

"Yeah, expected. I was being groomed for it from the time I was a little boy. Back then, sons of farmers were expected to be, well…farmers. You know, follow in your father's footsteps. That's just the way it was. It's not so much like that today, but that was the culture back then."

"I see." Diana put her hands down on the bed and leaned back. The siren in the distance was slowly dying away. "But farming has been very good to you. You have a good life."

I frowned and looked over at her. "Oh, I'm not arguing that. You're right. Farming has given me a good and comfortable life, and I'm proud to be in that profession. I'm not complaining about that. It's just that…well, it never was something that burned in my gut."

I stared at the carpet for a moment, collecting my thoughts. "So I guess that's why I'm not in such a hurry to go back, because I'm going back to something that, although I have done it all my life, it isn't *in* me, if you know what I mean. Am I making any sense?"

Diana looked at me silently for several seconds before she asked the unavoidable next question.

"What burned in your gut?"

I stood up and walked a few feet away from the bed. Turning around, I caught her eyes in mine again.

"Writing," I said.

"Writing?"

"Yes, writing. That's what I wanted to do. I wanted to be a journalist. I wanted to write for a newspaper, a magazine, whatever. Ever since about the sixth grade, that's what burned in my gut."

Diana sat on the edge of the bed, looking up at me, listening carefully to every word.

"But I couldn't do it," I continued. "Maybe it was just me, but I felt that I would have let my father down and my grandfather, too, if I had gone in any other direction than farming. I don't think they would have supported me being a writer. Silly, I know, but that's how I felt."

There was an uncomfortable silence as I stared at the wall, sorting through my feelings in that moment. Then I looked at Diana again. "And now both of them are dead and here I am, getting older by the day with regrets and unfulfilled dreams."

"I see," Diana said slowly. Then she abruptly looked up at me. "So fulfill them."

"What?'

"Fulfill them, your unfulfilled dreams. Write something."

I looked down at her flabbergasted. "How am I going to do that? I'm in my mid-fifties. I have no job in that area, no experience. What would I write?"

Diana was searching, looking down at the floor and thinking. "I don't know," she said. Then she looked up at me again as if a light bulb had just come on. "Write a book."

"A book? Oh come on. I wouldn't even know where to begin. And besides, what could I possibly write about that anybody would be interested in?"

"Well…I don't know. Why don't you write about what you're doing down here in Arizona?"

"What?"

"Write a book about what it's like to come down here to Arizona every winter. I bet there are lots of people who would like to know what that feels like."

I stood speechless as goose bumps rose on my arms.

Diana got up off the bed and walked over to me. "You can do anything you put your mind to, honey. You're a smart man. If you want to be a writer, you will be a writer."

She put her arms around my neck and kissed me softly on the lips.

"Now," she said, stepping back and poking a finger in my chest. "I want you to put your mind to getting packed. We've got a lot to do until tomorrow."

And she was gone, out the bedroom door and back to work.

My mind was racing a mile a minute. I turned around and grabbed an armload of clothing from the dresser drawer without stopping to see what I holding. *Write a book*, I said to myself. Plopping the clothes into the suitcase, I walked back to the dresser. My mind wandered again. *Write a book about snowbirds*. I reached into the drawer and grabbed up some more clothes.

The next morning dawned bright and clear, a beautiful Arizona spring day. Diana and I worked feverishly with an assortment of suitcases, boxes, and bags. After a couple of hours, we managed to push, prod, and shove everything into the car to make it fit.

"We got everything?" I asked, hands on my knees, huffing and puffing from all the exertion.

"I think so," replied Diana as she leaned against the wall of the garage trying to catch her breath.

"All right, then, I'm going up to the office and sign us out. When I get back, we'll leave." I walked out of the garage and headed for the clubhouse.

As I walked the familiar route, the heat of the sun warmed my shoulders. The cool weather up home was really going to take some getting used to. This Arizona sun had spoiled us. It will be a shock waking up for the first couple of days to the frosty April mornings that awaited us in Idaho. I shivered at the thought.

When I rounded the corner, I saw the old familiar figure of Virgil out doing his morning chores. His three-gallon tank filled with weed spray hanging loosely from his fingertips.

"Well now, why aren't you off to plant potatoes yet?" Virgil asked with a chuckle, his Minnesota accent hanging in the air as he sauntered over to the curb in his bent-over way.

I stopped and smiled at him. "We'll be leaving in a few minutes, Virgil."

He nodded his head and reached a bony hand up underneath his cap and scratched the side of his head. "I thought it was getting pretty close to potato planting time."

"Yeah, real close, Virgil. We'll be starting in about ten days or so. Then I'll be in a tractor for several weeks."

"Yes, you'll be real busy." His eyes left mine and he looked off into the distance. A smile slowly spread across his face as he looked over my shoulder at something that only he could see.

"I remember planting time was a special time," he said. "Get out of the house after being cooped up all winter. I couldn't wait till I was back out in the fields." He looked back at me and gave me a wink. "And neither could the missus."

We both chuckled. "Yeah, but now you got it easy, Virgil," I said. "I kind of envy you, all retired and everything, living down here in Arizona all year round."

Suddenly his facial expression dropped. His smile vanished. He squared himself towards me and stared into my face with a look of puzzlement. "Oh, that's where you got it all wrong," he said, shaking his head.

I took a step back. What did I say? Did I offend him? Did I make him mad?

Virgil moved toward me and put a gnarled hand, wrinkled with age, gently on my shoulder and smiled warmly into my eyes. "I would give anything to be back in your shoes," he said softly, lowering his voice. "You're young. You're doing something worthwhile. Me?" He turned and gestured at his yard. "I'm just out to pasture, biding my time." He turned back around and tapped a forefinger into my chest. "But you...you're still tilling the land."

He patted me on the shoulder and then started to walk away, looking for more phantom weeds among his red rocks. "No, you got it all backwards," he said, turning his head back to me again. "I'm the one who envies you."

With that, Virgil started his slow, methodical trek across his yard, staring intently at the ground, spray nozzle at the ready.

I didn't know how to react. Sheepishly, I waved at him. "Well, you take care, Virgil, see you next year."

He turned around and waved and flashed his friendly smile. "You drive safe now. Tell Diana goodbye from us."

"I will. Take care." I turned around and started walking again, a little smaller, a little humbler.

And all of a sudden...I couldn't wait to get home.

About the Author

Len Schritter and his wife Diana split their time between Aberdeen, Idaho, in the summer and Mesa, Arizona, in the winter. A third generation farmer and rancher, Len is in partnership with his brother on their 3,500-acre farm which produces Idaho potatoes, sugar beets, and wheat.

The Secret Life of a Snowbird is Len's first book. He is now at work on his second.